MW01108988

EASY WAYS TO SAVE AND MANAGE MONEY

—

A MONEY MANAGEMENT SYSTEM

4500 College Blvd. #180
Leawood, KS 66211
1/888/888-7696

CONTENTS

PART I
GETTING READY

PART II
SUBJECTS THAT WILL PROVIDE A
FOUNDATION OF KNOWLEDGE TO
HELP YOUR MONEY MANAGEMENT
PLANNING

PART III
EXAMPLES OF OPPORTUNITIES
TO CONTROL EXPENSES —
HELP IN MAKING DECISIONS

PART VI
SPECIAL SUBJECTS OF INTEREST
TO SOME READERS —

PART VII
THE GRAND FINALE

JAMES H. METZGER INTRODUCES THE AUTHOR

It has been my good fortune to observe Tom Schwartz in action for most of the last fifty years.

Tom Schwartz

These observations got a big boost when I had the privilege of being a member of his "team" in his role as the chairman of the inaugural of Robert Docking as the governor of Kansas in 1971. At that time I was the vice president of corporate relations at the Security Benefit Group of Cos.

At the first meeting of his "team" Tom stated, "We want this inaugural to be the *best* Kansas has ever had." The goal was achieved with many features including the first statewide telecast. That is a typical goal for Tom on any project, including this book, that he undertakes.

Tom had the same high standards as the chairman of the Greater Topeka Chamber of Commerce and president of the Native Sons of Kansas.

Among other notable achievements, he has served as a chairman, director, consultant, worker and contributor to many fund-raising campaigns for a wide range of worthy causes.

He has served on the board of directors of the United Way of Greater Topeka, Jayhawk Area Council of The Boy Scouts of America, Campfire Girls, and St. Francis Health Center.

3

In 1993 the Topeka Community Foundation recognized Tom and his wife for their Distinguished Leadership in Philanthropy. In 1997 he received the Capper Foundation's highest award and in 1998 was named the Sales and Marketing Executive of the Year. He was recently named The Volunteer of the Year for 2002 by the Junior League of Topeka.

At what Tom likes to call his "tender age of 89," he has had a lifetime of observing a wide assortment of wise and unwise things people do in money management.

He gives credit to his father for the first lesson. His father was a banker in Paola, Kansas, a city largely dependent on the agricultural economy. All of the United States was hit by the stock market crash and Great Depression starting in 1929. Many people, primarily farmers, were losing their properties through foreclosure of mortgages as a result of going into debt too easily when times were good.

Tom's first lesson from his father was that it is easier to go into debt than to work yourself out of debt. He stressed the importance of a borrower having a solid plan for repaying a loan.

When Tom graduated from high school in 1931, the Great Depression was in full swing. It seemed that everyone was hurting financially. Tom felt he should work his way through college rather than put that burden on his father.

He attended Rockhurst University in Kansas City for two years and then headed east to Washington, D.C., to attend Georgetown University Law School.

He became a government clerk, with beginning pay of $115 per month, on the midnight shift of the Reconstruction Finance Corporation.

It had been started by President Herbert Hoover to loan money to banks all over the United States to enable them to remain in business while their debtors needed more time to pay off loans they had obtained from the banks. Tom's father's bank did not have to use this governmental aid.

Tom's next lessons in money management came from his fellow government clerks. It seemed that most of them were constantly having a hard time getting by financially. Tom became a counselor to many of them. In the process, he learned much from their mistakes.

It was at this time he started his "Four-S System: Save Some, Spend Some," which he suggests for children and adults in a chapter in this book.

Tom did so by mailing his paycheck to his bank with instructions for some of it to first be placed in a savings account and the balance to be placed in a checking account.

After graduating from Georgetown and passing the bar exam, Tom decided to join the practice of law in Kansas City with an older brother.

He quickly learned some new lessons on the need for frugality in living on his compensation of $50 per month, which was the current compensation for a beginning lawyer.

After a year, he returned to Washington as an attorney for the Securities and Exchange Commission. At the SEC, Tom learned one of his pet bits of advice. He and his boss became good friends and socialized together but with the boss having much higher compensation. The boss would sometimes say something like, "Let's do something next Wednesday." Tom would inquire, "Why Wednesday?" The boss would reply, "Because that's payday."

That was the beginning of Tom's admonition to discipline yourselves so you can afford to buy something just as easily on the day *before* payday as you can on payday.

In his first year in the Navy in World War II, Tom served as a counter-intelligence agent but seldom wearing a uniform. He moved from that into Navy flying, where he got his "wings" and then became a flight instructor, crash investigator and safety officer "selling" safety. He moved upward to the position of assistant superintendent of aviation training at a Naval Air Station with responsibility for the ground school and flight line. He retired as a lieutenant commander.

It was as a crash investigator that Tom developed a standard of performance. He was in the process of signing crash investigation reports that would be forwarded to an admiral in Washington. He noticed the typing was not satisfactory and asked his secretary how she felt about her work. She replied, "I thought the work was average and good enough to get by."

6

Tom immediately adopted a new standard, which he has followed in the business world since World War II. That policy is: "It is not sufficient for our work to be average or good enough to get by. It must be above average and of which we can be justifiably proud."

For more than 50 years, he served as the head of a very successful distributing company with more than 100 employees. Tom decided to call members of his "team" associates rather than employees. He has always had a personal interest in the financial well-being of his associates. To many of them he was pleased to serve as a financial counselor. Many times it was a matter of helping them devise a plan where they could work themselves out of financial difficulties.

Tom suffers from poor eyesight as a result of macular degeneration. He has had to use magnifying projectors to write and edit this book. The book has thus become a "labor of love," which he hopes will help many people.

Tom and his wife, Helen, have contributed the first 10,000 copies and all future rights to this book to the Topeka Community Foundation to support their many worthy causes. The Foundation will work with publishers in achieving national distribution.

James H. Metzger

FOREWORD AND ACKNOWLEDGMENTS

We are pleased to present our planned second edition on individual and family financial management. This follows our 1998 book, *Family Budgeting, Highly Rewarding Decisions.*

As that book was completed, we decided not to have it published and offered for sale but to use it as a research project for this book. We had 10,000 copies printed, and they were given to a wide range of readers with a definite purpose.

We wanted the readers to know we were planning a second edition and wanted their suggestions on improvements. We wanted their suggestions on subjects to be retained or improved and new subjects they felt would be of value to readers.

Our goal was to receive a broad representation of suggestions and ideas from individuals and types of families in all income levels.

Five thousand copies were distributed to Boy Scouts and their families. Three thousand five hundred copies were distributed to Junior Achievement to assist them in their training of young people. We wanted to get input from the Junior Achievement staff, the dedicated volunteers who conduct their training and the young trainees and their families.

Books also were distributed through the YMCA, YWCA, Salvation Army and a wide range of other organizations. Hundreds of copies were given to business friends who expressed interest in making them available to their employees and families.

Most of the readers were given a postage-paid survey form on which they could give us their thoughts without disclosing names or any identification.

The response was excellent, and we received a tremendous amount of valued input. Suggestions from members of our family, business associates, bankers, business friends and countless others were very helpful. All suggestions were carefully considered and led to many improvements in this edition.

Professionals in various fields accepted our invitations to write chapters on important subjects. Those subjects were designed to provide a "foundation of knowledge" for those planning a money management system. Names and biographical information on the special authors are provided at the beginning of their chapters.

While my name appears as the author of this book, it would be more appropriate to describe me as a collector of ideas from many sources.

It is difficult for any one person to take credit for an original idea on money management. An idea is passed from one person to another, expanding as it passes along. In time the idea loses the identity of the original source. Wherever possible, we have attempted to give credit for the original sources of ideas.

It is appropriate I express my first appreciation for assistance on this book to my wife, Helen, for her cooperation and ideas through the years. This goes back to the starting of our personal family money management system, which we developed shortly after we were married. This was presented in my first book, *My Best*, published in 1990.

We were privileged in the preparation of this edition to have the assistance of several highly qualified individuals:

—— Karen Hiller, Kansas Executive Director, Housing and Credit Counseling Inc. and their affiliate, Consumer Credit Counseling Service based in Topeka, and her staff helped in many ways.

They are affiliated with a worldwide not-for-profit organization, the National Foundation for Credit Counseling, with offices in many cities in the United States and foreign countries. This organization is truly in a class by itself in the services it provides in helping people with personal and family financial management. They provide educational guidance and then professional assistance when individuals and families become so overburdened they cannot master their problems by themselves.

Special recognition and appreciation is extended to Don Mitts of the Topeka office. Robert Baker of the Lawrence office was also very helpful. Without disclosing names or other identifying information, this group provided many insights into the problems people face in developing money management systems and overcoming difficulties.

—— Linda Smith, regional director of Junior Achievement in Northeast Kansas, provided counsel and advice that was helpful in many ways. Her staff organizes and supervises volunteer teachers from a wide variety of professions and businesses. They teach the fundamentals of money management to children through elementary and high school years. The volunteers conduct training sessions over many weeks, with many of the volunteers providing this important service for several years.

One such volunteer is John P. Hamilton, a practicing attorney in Topeka. He provided valuable insights to the needs of people who are planning money management. We are honored that our book *Family Budgeting — Highly Rewarding Decisions* has been used in this training program.

We express our appreciation to Steve Clinkinbeard, longtime managing partner of BCC Business Services, Inc., a CPA firm. He has served us for many years as an upper-level business consultant on a wide variety of subjects. Special recognition goes to Denise Peterson and Mike Schirmer, both CPAs with the firm, for outstanding contributions in several chapters, including the preparation of statistical charts throughout the book.

One of their important contributions is the chapter on the tax benefits available from setting money aside for future college educations. They also assisted in developing a plan for setting aside and investing money that will be needed, over and above Social Security and other income, in your retirement years.

—— Robert Hull, Ph.D., a professor of finance at Washburn University School of Business in Topeka, provided counsel and advice that was very helpful.

—— Jim Hanni, President of AAA Kansas, was very helpful in enlisting the excellent cooperatioin of the AAA National Staff in providing valuable statistical data in the Automobile chapter which will be helpful to our readers.

—— Diana Carlin, Ph.D., dean of the Graduate School at The University of Kansas, played a valued role in the early planning of the book.

—— My longtime friend, Jim Metzger, was very helpful as a consultant and was very kind in his introduction of the author.

—— Several associates, including Gary Rexford, Belinda Roberts, Amanda Bunting, LeRoy Haug and Douglas Worswick provided a variety of services. To Kelly Adams goes special credit for the final editing of the text. We particularly salute Julie Howbert for great work and dedication in improving the text through several stages.

To all who have contributed to our efforts, we express our heartiest gratitude. We hope all of our readers will benefit from the contributions of these dedicated people.

Tom Schwartz

PREFACE

In the course of writing about personal and family financial planning, we have tried to capture the best approach to the subject. We previously wrote of the budgeting process, but now we approach it as a money management system.

The word "budget" frequently sounds like work, while "money management" is more enjoyable, rewarding and challenging. If you can develop that feeling, your money management will be a rewarding experience, and your life and the lives of your family will be much happier.

Our company placed "table tent" signs on the desks of our managers to remind them of something they should do to improve their performance. One such message symbolizes the challenges in this book!

> *No one plans to fail.*
> *Some just fail to plan.*

The importance of planning is also expressed by the "Five P's" developed by Dr. Roy Abbott, a psychologist:
Prior Planning Prevents Poor Performance.

Planning is what this book is all about.

Our Money Management System is designed to help individuals and families in all income levels who want to live happily within their incomes, thus preventing the family discord and unhappiness that frequently occurs if family finances are not under control.

As we introduce our management system it is important to point out it is not suggested only for households of married couples with children.

The system is suggested for teenagers, single adults, young couples with no children, couples with children, single parents and seniors who still need to do financial planning in their lives. *That requires you to adapt the plan to your lifestyle and situations.*

Even in husband, wife and children lifestyles you need to adapt the use of your abilities to achieve maximum benefits. Let the wife or husband lead to achieve the best results.

Singles and single parents may need to develop special approaches to cover all of the subjects.

Think of our plan as a general plan that you can improve by making changes that fit your lifestyle.

There is no "magic wand" or "fast fix" in developing ways to manage personal or family finances, but it is certainly not impossible. It takes common sense, simple arithmetic and determination. The first two will come easily. Determination will be the most difficult, but it will be worth the effort. *The hours spent developing a money management system can be the most rewarding hours of your lives.*

16

The book is divided into seven parts.

Part I encourages you to develop the right attitude and challenges you to develop a money management system.

Part II contains an assortment of chapters that provide a foundation of knowledge that will be helpful in planning your system.

Part III addresses a wide range of spending decisions all people face at one time or another.

Part IV gives you a preview of our recommended use of accrual accounts and multiple bank accounts in monitoring your progress.

Part V acquaints you with the Monthly Money Management Goals Form. It helps you organize past financial information and explains the steps needed to prepare your Maximum Spending Goals for the future.

It then shows how bank accounts can help monitor your progress. If you need further help, a Goals Monitoring Procedure is presented. An Envelope System is also presented as a possible necessity for some families.

Part VI presents a system for reducing debts and avoiding bankruptcy. It challenges you to put forth extra effort to increase your income as an important step in your money management. Suggestions on where to get additional assistance, if your financial affairs have reached the

crisis stage and professional counseling is needed, are also presented.

Part VII presents *The Grand Finale* — How You Can Save Here and There and Become A Millionaire. This series of charts reminds you of the savings you can achieve and the benefits of depositing and investing the savings.

Our hope is that you will benefit from the experiences of those who have contributed to this book. We have recognized previously that it is difficult to present a completely new idea in family money management. Against that background, we are presenting a method and ideas we feel are new or new to the extent that we feature them.

We suggest the money management system be divided into six accounts to make it easier to plan and track the various necessary steps. We recommend separate bank accounts to go with each management account to make it easier to track your progress.

We recommend accrual type accounts, where you plan future expenditures and then build up funds in those accounts in advance so you will have money on hand when those planned purchases become expenses.

Throughout the book there will be many charts based on interest paid on indebtedness and interest received on savings. The rates used have been the prevailing rates in the past 10 years in the United States. Rates at any time are based on the general financial condition of the country. The important points will be the *lessons to be learned* rather than the exact amount involved in the specific illustration.

The purpose of this book is not to tell you how you should lead your lives or spend your money. It is to present choices so you can make the wisest decisions in meeting your financial goals and ensuring family accord and happiness.

Tom Schwartz

PART I
GETTING READY

OPENING THE DOORS OF OPPORTUNITIES

$ $ $ REWARDS $ $ $

$34,812	$195,378	$76,619
HUNDREDS OF THOUSANDS OF DOLLARS IN REWARDS FOR YOU.		
Everyone is eligible	No advance cash is required	
Here's how you can win!		
$226,782	$153,238	$306,476

We think many people when they first see the above chart will say to themselves, "That doesn't apply to us."

But it does! It applies to everyone, and we want you to get your share. You won't have to gamble or take a chance. Just take advantage of the opportunities! Each of the dollar amounts on the above chart has a special significance for *you* that will be explained later.

Albert Einstein is honored as one of the most important persons in American history. He was a brilliant man and noted for his contributions in several fields. He was a scientist, a mathematician, an important contributor to the electronic age, a contributor to mastering the atom and much more.

One of his most important statements was — *"The compounding of interest is the strongest force in the universe."*

22

The dictionary defines compounding as the earning of interest on principal plus interest that was earned previously.

Compounding can also be described as the process which computes and adds interest on the original principal and then continues to add this interest to the principal balance for future calculations and additions.

The frequency of compounding is very important. For example, compounding monthly will result in larger amounts than compounding annually.

With the following chart on The Magic of Compounding — The Master Chart on How Money "Grows" — we hope to impress you with the benefits of cutting expenses and saving money and the long-term financial benefits for you from doing so.

The key to financial success lies in the magic of compounding. Make *your* dreams come true!

THE MAGIC OF COMPOUNDING — THE MASTER CHART ON HOW MONEY "GROWS"

These projections demonstrate how an amount saved and deposited or invested and compounded monthly, at 5 percent per year, will grow.

Monthly deposit or investment	Will grow to these amounts in the years indicated					
	5	10	20	30	40	50
$25	$1,707	$3,898	$10,319	$20,893	$38,309	$66,994
$50	$3,414	$7,796	$20,638	$41,787	$76,619	$133,989
$75	$5,122	$11,695	$30,956	$62,680	$114,928	$200,983
$100	$6,829	$15,593	$41,275	$83,574	$153,238	$267,977
$200	$13,658	$31,186	$82,551	$167,148	$306,476	$535,954
$300	$20,487	$46,779	$123,826	$250,722	$459,714	$803,931
$400	$27,316	$62,372	$165,101	$334,295	$612,951	$1,071,908
$500	$34,145	$77,965	$206,377	$417,869	$766,189	$1,339,886

The passing of time and the number of years involved will provide a very important role in helping your money "grow."

Few people can "jump start" a savings or investment plan with a large amount of money. Everyone else has to do it gradually, down to a few dollars at a time. The passage of time creates big benefits for you.

Start to save as much as possible at the earliest possible age. If you start early, the results will be almost beyond belief. If you wait too long, you will never catch up with what you might have otherwise accomplished.

Study carefully The Master Chart On How Money "Grows" to get a solid understanding.

The No. 1 objective of this book is to assist every individual, couple or family develop a feeling of security through their money management system.

The first and most important factor in the system is to spend your money carefully and wisely and thus develop some net savings from your income. The next important factor is to deposit the savings achieved and place them in a savings account or investment *every month*, where they can grow and continue to increase your feeling of security.

Think of *every* type of expense as a prospect for savings. Later in the book will be many examples of small, medium and large expenses that can be avoided or reduced and produce great benefits. A pack of cigarettes per day or one or two cans of pop will serve as examples.

In the chapter "Teaching Children Money Management," we will be presenting the Four "S" System — Save Some, Spend Some — to encourage *children* and *everyone* to *first* save some of any money which comes into their possession and then spend some.

We hope the Master Chart will give you determination in developing your money management system so you can achieve the goal spelled out in the last chapter of this book — "How You Can Save Here and There and Become A Millionaire."

25

ENCOURAGEMENT AND CHALLENGES

If you are discouraged because of the problems of family money management, we hope you will find encouragement in the words of famous people from centuries and times past.

Confucius lived about 500 BC and his words were — *"He who will not economize will have to agonize."*

Benjamin Franklin lived from 1706 to 1790 and his words were — *"Beware of little expenses: A small leak will sink a great ship."*

John D. Rockefeller lived from 1839 to 1937. He was described as "going from rags to billions." He said a money management system is a "must." His words were — *"Write it down so you can see it."*

The old Chinese proverb from Lao-Tsu (605-531 BC) is very much in point — *"A journey of a thousand miles must begin with a single step."*

RECOGNIZING THE NEED TO MAKE DECISIONS

The most important factor in money management is recognizing you have to make choices about what you can or cannot afford, whatever your income level might be. This may be the most important challenge in this book.

There is no person on earth who can afford everything he or she desires. Most people seem to have a desire to have something they cannot afford. The world's wealthiest persons might wish they could take a trip to the planet Mars but can't afford it. We all need to be *realistic* about what we can afford.

People with low incomes have many tough decisions to make. But people with higher incomes think their decisions are also tough. No one has an "easy go," but some make it easier and prove the value of having a money management system.

No one at any income level can escape the necessity of making decisions. The secret to mastering money problems lies in facing those decisions, knowing that some will be easy and some will be difficult or very difficult.

The first step in controlling your finances is acknowledging the need to quietly examine your spending patterns and the choices you need to make.

27

DEVELOPING THE RIGHT ATTITUDE

As you start to work on your money management system, you first need to develop the right attitude.

Successful baseball players don't just walk from the dugout to home plate and start swinging the bat, hoping for a hit. Days before a game, the players know who the opposing pitcher is going to be. They get all of the information they can about what the pitcher will be throwing their way. On game day, before it is time to bat, they watch the pitcher to get a fresh look at the challenges they are going to face.

Between the dugout and home plate they go through a ritual of getting themselves ready. They select a bat and swing it a few times to make sure it has the right "feel." They tug at their uniforms here and there to make sure they feel comfortable. Then they seem to clear all other matters out of their minds as they step to the plate. Their apparent attitude is — *"I am ready to do what is necessary."*

Go through similar mental steps as you get ready to tackle the money management challenge. Developing the right mental attitude is the first step in good financial planning.

In getting some business expenses in line, a company came up with these words —

> *Economizing is a state of mind that produces good results.*

If you can get with the spirit of economizing, make tough decisions and determine to live within your income, the rest will come easy (or at least easier). You may not have to economize down to the last penny, but you do need to get with a system and make it work.

WHAT IS ESSENTIAL AND WHAT IS DISCRETIONARY— NEEDS VS. WANTS

In relation to the money management process, ESSENTIAL is defined in the dictionary as "indispensable, *necessary*, of the utmost importance." DISCRETIONARY is defined as "the making of responsible decisions, a *choice* or judgment."

Discretionary expenses are for items people *can* live without, such as expensive jewelry. Essential expenses are for things such as food, shelter and clothing. But keep in mind that even among *essential* items there are many *discretionary* decisions.

There are many levels of quality and prices for food, clothes, shelter and many other items. Wisely deciding what to purchase can reduce your expenses and stretch your dollars. This requires very careful analysis. Be tough on yourselves as you start to make decisions.

Sometimes purchases that seem satisfying at the moment do not hold their appeal very long, and occasionally you may regret making a purchase after you've thought it over. Ask yourselves when facing the wide variety of opportunities to spend money: *"Is this item clearly ESSENTIAL? Or should it be considered DISCRETIONARY?"*

Deciding on the degree of essential and discretionary will be a tough but very important part of your financial planning. As you work your way through the *Monthly Money Management Goals Form* in Part V, you will constantly face that question. There will be many moments of decision. That's what money management is all about!

Before purchasing discretionary items, compare the pleasure of purchasing the item to the pleasure you will derive by putting all or part of that money into a savings account or investment where it will grow and be rewarding to you in the future. Ask yourselves which you would rather have — pleasure in the present or the *big pleasure* in the future?

You will be frequently facing the questions of what is "essential" and what is "discretionary" as you work your way through your money management system.

PART II
SUBJECTS THAT WILL PROVIDE
A FOUNDATION OF KNOWLEDGE
TO HELP YOUR *MONEY*
MANAGEMENT PLANNING

THE ROLE OF BANKS IN YOUR MONEY MANAGEMENT SYSTEM

PATRICK "PAT" W. MICHAELIS

Pat Michaelis has had a distinguished career in banking since graduating from The University of Kansas and the Graduate School of Banking at the University of Wisconsin.

With broad experience in the fundamentals of banking, he has progressed to top executive positions in small, medium and large banks, including being president of Bank IV in Hutchinson, Kansas, and Bank of America in Topeka, Kansas. He is now the Director of Development, Eastern United States, for Kansas State University.

He has also made important contributions to the following two chapters.

Let's get acquainted with the departments and functions of a bank.

CHECKING AND SAVINGS ACCOUNTS

As you enter the bank to open an account, there will be someone to direct you to the New Accounts desk. Let's assume that your first account as an adult will be a checking account.

The bank representative will explain that the bank has different types of checking accounts with various amounts of beginning deposits required, the service charges involved based on the balance carried and number of checks written in a month.

As you open a checking account, you probably will start with a deposit and possibly have some service charges. If you carry a minimum balance, there probably will be no service charge. After getting all of the facts, you can select the accounts that best fit your needs.

Sooner or later, you will want to open one or more savings accounts. The bank representative will tell you about the various types of savings accounts they have, the opening deposit required and the interest that will be paid on your balance. In a following chapter is a chart showing minimum deposits required and service charges that might be involved.

You might eventually arrange for a certificate of deposit (C.D.) at the bank. A certificate of deposit is another form of a savings account. In arranging for a C.D., you will make a deposit of a certain amount, which you agree to keep in the bank for a stated period of time. You generally will earn a higher interest rate on a C.D. than is normally paid on a standard savings account. Generally, the longer the deposit is committed, the higher the interest rate. Because there is usually a penalty charged for an early withdrawal, you must plan ahead and be certain a C.D. fits your money management plan.

BANK ACCOUNT TRANSACTIONS

After you have opened an account or accounts, you can complete future transactions at a teller window in the bank or a drive-through window at the bank or branches.

Most banks also have ATM facilities (automated teller machines), where you can secure cash withdrawals from your account and make deposits. There is usually a charge for this service. Many banks have multiple locations for your convenience.

You also can make deposits by mail. Some employers will transmit your compensation directly to the bank. Your deposits can be made to your checking account or divided as you desire between your checking and savings accounts.

Most banks feature automatic debits from your checking account for making payments on your real estate and other loan payments and utility bills. This ensures the payments will be

35

made on time. It also can be a convenience for you.

Banks are generally competitive on their service charges and rates of interest paid, but it is always good business to reassure yourselves you are getting the best possible rates.

All banks now are required to carry deposit insurance with the Federal Deposit Insurance Corporation, and the balance of your total accounts is guaranteed up to $100,000.

CREDIT CARDS AND DEBIT CARDS

Banks act as the agent for major credit card companies like Visa and Mastercard. You make an application for a card, and the bank sends it to the credit card company for approval and the issuance of a card subject to the amount of credit being authorized and the payment and interest terms prescribed. Payments are made to the credit card company and not to the bank from which you received the card.

A debit card is issued by a bank to a customer who has deposited designated money in the bank. The funds placed in the customer's account may come from a loan secured from the bank.

A debit card is used to make a purchase instead of writing a check for the amount. With the debit card, the amount is immediately deducted from the customer's bank balance.

If a credit card is used, the credit card company, in effect, loans the cardholder the amount of the purchase until the first of the following month. A minimum payment on the credit card is due every month, and there is an interest charge on any unpaid balance. There will be more information in a later chapter on credit cards.

LOANS

There are other departments of the bank that will have services of interest to you. If your credit is good, a personal loan can be obtained at the bank for an automobile, home improvement or other needs.

Banks make both secured and unsecured loans. If you have a steady source of income and a good credit record, a bank may make you an unsecured loan without specific collateral such as stocks and bonds. This would generally be for a period from one month to two years or so, probably with payments due each month. This type of loan requires only a signature.

The amount at which a bank will loan on an unsecured basis depends on the income, net worth and credit record of the prospective borrower. One guideline, sometimes followed by banks, is to loan up to 10 percent of the applicant's net worth.

On other loans the bank may require collateral. This might involve pledging your automobile, a C.D. or other assets such as stocks or bonds to assure the bank you will make payments when due.

Factors that will be considered by a bank in making you a secured or unsecured loan will be your income as an individual or couple, your total amount of indebtedness as compared to your total assets, *your record of making payments on all debts when due* and your record, if any, regarding having checks to a store or other payee returned because of insufficient funds in your bank account.

Another important department of the bank is the real estate loan department. This is where the bank will process your request to purchase a home secured by a mortgage, or perhaps later, a home equity loan. The total amount that a bank will loan on a home is generally competitive between banks and other financial institutions. The interest rate and charges for the loan are also competitive.

The amount that will be loaned to you will be based on your income, credit record and your ability to make the payments on time.

The banks and other financial institutions will make a careful study of your ability to make your payments on time. It is also very important, when borrowing money, that *you* are *certain* you can make the payments when due. *It has been demonstrated many times that it is much easier to get into debt than it is to get out of debt.*

Many people make the mistake of thinking that if they can borrow or charge a certain amount of money, it is a sign they can afford the object they are buying. That is not so. The test is whether people can afford a certain item, not that there is easy credit to make the purchase possible.

A very important loan department of a bank is the commercial loans department for individual, partnership or corporate businesses. These loans can vary from a few hundred to thousands of dollars for a small business just starting, to many millions of dollars for large businesses.

Some of the larger loans might be used to provide necessary machinery or equipment, finance an inventory or provide funds to carry accounts receivable until customers pay their debts.

EQUIPMENT LEASES

Banks also can buy and lease equipment to you such as automobiles and computer equipment used for business purposes.

SAFETY DEPOSIT BOXES

You also might wish to rent a safety deposit box from a bank. These metal fireproof boxes are maintained in the bank vault, with the bank having one key to the box and you having a key. It takes both keys to open the box. The bank has a private room for you to review the items in your box.

You might wish to keep items like birth certificates, insurance policies, certificates of deposit, stocks and bonds, important contracts or jewelry in a safety deposit box.

TRUST DEPARTMENT

Another very important department of the bank is the trust department. A trust department can be named as the executor, the manager of your estate. Another service might be to administer and perform duties in fulfilling a formal contract, a trust, for financial services.

A trust generally provides for the bank trust department to manage assets placed in their custody with the proceeds to be distributed in the manner you specify. Lawyers prepare these documents. There are fees for these services, and the bank trust department performs the specified services for a specified fee.

INVESTMENTS

Many banks now also have investment departments where you can buy and sell stocks and bonds or arrange for your IRA (individual retirement account).

INSURANCE

A growing number of banks have an insurance department where you can buy many types of insurance.

Over a period of time you probably will use most of the departments of the bank.

THE EASE IN OPENING
BANK ACCOUNTS

In our research concerning this book we told many people of our approach to money management. This involves six bank accounts to help monitor spending through money management accounts which replace the old-fashioned budget.

Some people expressed concern about possible difficulty in opening and having that many accounts. We want to remove any concerns you might have.

At this point we will only touch on the ease of opening the accounts. Later in the book we will tell you how the bank accounts will make your money management system better and easier for you.

The thought of having six bank accounts might seem overwhelming until you understand the function of the accounts. There will be only two active checking accounts. The other accounts will basically be savings or limited action checking accounts with a deposit each month and a few withdrawals in the course of a year.

By having these separate accounts, the bank will do much record-keeping for you that you would otherwise have to do yourselves.

So relax and don't worry about the bank accounts. We are confident you will receive many benefits from the bank accounts in the future.

Later in the book we will be presenting the Money Management Accounts. This will be followed by explanations of how bank accounts will fit those management accounts.

INFORMATION AND SUGGESTED QUESTIONS IN SELECTING THE BEST BANK OR BANKS FOR YOU

On the next two pages we will give you the basic information required by banks when you open checking and savings accounts. These charts summarize information from four banks. One chart covers information on checking accounts, and the other chart covers savings accounts.

Checking Account Examples

	BANK A	BANK B	BANK C	BANK D
MINIMUM DEPOSIT FOR OPENING CHECKING ACCOUNT	$100	$100	$100	$100
MINIMUM BALANCE REQUIRED FOR A NO FEE CHARGE	$200	$500	$500	$500
MONTHLY SERVICE CHARGE FOR ACCOUNT UNDER MINIMUM BALANCE	$5	$5	$6	$6
QUANTITY OF CHECKS THAT CAN BE WRITTEN PER MONTH	20 CHECKS. AFTER 20 CHECKS .30 PER CHECK	40 CHECKS. AFTER 40 CHECKS, .25 PER CHECK	UNLIMITED	UNLIMITED

Note: If you maintain the minimum balance, the bank will pay you interest.

Savings Account Examples

	BANK A	BANK B	BANK C	BANK D
MINIMUM DEPOSIT FOR OPENING SAVINGS ACCOUNT	$100	$100	$100	$100
MINIMUM BALANCE REQUIRED FOR A NO FEE CHARGE	$300	$300	$300	$300
MONTHLY SERVICE CHARGE FOR ACCOUNT UNDER MINIMUM BALANCE	$5	$3	$3	$3
MINIMUM DEPOSIT FOR OPENING SAVINGS ACCOUNT FOR PERSONS UNDER 18 YEARS OF AGE	$5	$25	$25	$25
MINIMUM BALANCE REQUIRED	NONE	NONE	NONE	NONE
SERVICE CHARGES OR FEES	NONE	NONE	NONE	NONE
WITHDRAWLS ALLOWED	3 PER MONTH AFTER 3 .75 EACH	2 PER MONTH AFTER 2 .75 EACH	3 PER QUARTER AFTER 3 .75 EACH	3 PER QUARTER AFTER 3 $1.00 EACH

Keep these accounts in mind as you consider a bank or banks you might use in your money management system.

43

QUESTIONS TO ASK BANKS

1. What types of checking accounts do you have from the standpoint of the minimum deposit required to open the account, any minimum balance required and the service charges involved for various numbers of checks written? Are there any other requirements or charges on checking accounts of which we should be aware? Do you have interest-bearing checking accounts? How do they work?

2. We understand that writing a check for more money than we have in the account is called an "overdraft." We plan to prevent any overdrafts, but we want to know what might be involved if we make a mistake. Do you have overdraft insurance in case we write a check when we do not have sufficient funds in our account? What is the cost of the overdraft insurance? If we do not have overdraft insurance, what charge would there be by the bank if we happen to have an overdraft? We are aware a store or any other payee makes a charge when an insufficient check is returned to them.

3. What types of savings accounts do you have? What is the minimum deposit required to open a savings account? Is there a minimum amount required to make additional deposits from time to time? What withdrawals from a savings account are permitted? What interest is paid on a savings account? How often is the interest computed and added to the balance

of the account? Are there any charges in connection with a savings account of which we should be aware?

4. What are the rates of interest you pay on certificates of deposit for various periods of time? What penalty would there be if we cashed our C.D. before its maturity date? Can we borrow against our C.D.?

5. Do you have automatic teller machines, and what charges are there for using them to make cash withdrawals?

6. What credit cards do you issue, and what are the annual fees? What is the interest rate on any balance due after payment of the minimum payment each month?

7. Do you issue debit cards? How do they work, and what are the charges for using them?

8. What rate of interest do you charge on personal loans, automobile loans, home mortgage loans and home equity loans?

9. How does one begin to establish credit? How might a co-signer help?

10. Do you have transaction charges on deposits, withdrawals, ATMs or others we should know about?

11. Can we have direct deposits from our employers for our paychecks?

12. Do you have safe deposit boxes? What are the charges?

13. We would like to have the benefit of financial advice from time to time. Would a bank officer be available to confer with us?

14. Do you offer online banking?

15. Do you offer 24-hour banking where I can access account information any time?

The banks want to have you as a customer. Feel free to ask any other questions you have.

TEACHING CHILDREN MONEY MANAGEMENT

A Collection of Ideas

> *This chapter is presented with deep appreciation to many parents who shared their favorite ideas on teaching children money management.*

Teaching children the fundamentals of money management, which they can use their entire lives, is one of the greatest gifts parents can give their children. This should start at the earliest possible age.

THE "FOUR-'S' SYSTEM"

In the first lesson on money management, candy might be used as a symbol for money when the child is old enough to enjoy candy. When interest in candy is expressed, give the child two pieces with encouragement to *save* one for *later* and one to *enjoy now*.

This is the introduction to the *"Four-'S' System"* — *Save Some, Spend Some* — that can be the "guiding light" for the child in a lifetime of money management.

The purpose is to teach children to *save* a percent of any money that is given to them or that they earn. There will be more about the "Four-'S' System" later.

THE "PIGGY BANK" ERA

Here is a good beginning point! As soon as children get their piggy bank, give them some coins with the understanding they will first *save* some coins in their piggy bank and then buy something with the balance of the coins.

The child can have the pleasure of putting coins in the piggy bank many times and shaking the piggy bank to hear the noise of the coins inside.

MONEY WILL "GROW"

The next step is to introduce the child to the fact the money will not "grow" in the piggy bank, but will "grow" if the money is taken to that *big* bank in that *big* building.

Explain to the child the people at the *big* bank will hold and protect the money and pay him or her interest for using the money until the child wants it back.

Interest is money paid for using money. If you deposit money in a savings account, the bank pays you interest. When a bank loans you money, you pay the bank interest on your loan.

When the piggy bank gets somewhat filled, it will be time to take the money out of the piggy bank and take it to the *big* bank to open a savings account.

Parents need to understand *compounding of interest* on savings as the first step in passing that knowledge on to their children.

Banks pay interest for the use of money placed in their custody. The bank then loans it at a higher rate to other customers and thus makes a profit for the bank.

As previously stated, compounding is the earning of interest on interest previously earned and added to the savings account. Compounding continues to add a new total again and again. Compounding can be based on any set period of time such as annually, semi-annual-ly, monthly or any specified period of time. Compounding is very advantageous when you are *receiving* its benefits.

The following chart presents the simple exam-ple of $500 being deposited in a savings account at 6 percent interest per year, compounded annually.

HOW MONEY "GROWS" AT 6% COMPOUNDED ANNUALLY	
Original Deposit	$500.00
Interest Earned in 1st Year	$ 30.00
New Balance at End of Year 1	$530.00
Interest Earned on New Balance	$ 31.80
New Balance at End of Year 2	$561.80
Interest Earned on New Balance	$ 33.71
New Balance at End of Year 3	$595.51

When opening a savings account, take the child to the *big* bank. Explain to him or her what a savings account is, what a bank teller does and such terms as "deposit," "withdrawal," "earned interest" and *very importantly*, the benefits of "compounding" as an example of how money "grows."

It will be difficult at first for a child to under-stand how interest is paid on savings accounts and how interest is compounded. Children will have difficulty understanding compounding, so the lesson will need to be repeated several times.

The seeds of small flowers planted in a pot will help deliver the message that money does "grow." Just take a small flowerpot, fill it with soil, buy a small package of flower seeds and plant the seeds. Add water and sunshine, and let the child enjoy watching the flowers grow. Explain that his or her savings account is growing like the flowers.

The following chart also illustrates how money will grow for the benefit of a child. The parents may start an account of from $100 to $500, for example, to celebrate the arrival of a new son or daughter and let that amount grow until the child reaches his or her 21st birthday. The figures show the growth of that account in 21 years.

HOW MONEY CAN GROW
FROM BIRTH TO 21 YEARS

BEGINNING DEPOSIT AT BIRTH	$100	$200	$300	$400	$500
In 21 years at 6% compounded monthly the amount at age 21 will be —	$351.44	$702.88	$1,054.32	$1,405.76	$1,757.20

The next chart shows the "real life" benefits of saving and compounding money from age 3 to age 21.

MONEY DOES "GROW"
A SAVINGS ACCOUNT OPENED WITH $100 AT AGE 3 AND ADDED TO WITH INCREASING MONTHLY DEPOSITS AT VARIOUS AGES, ALL COMPOUNDED MONTHLY AT 6%, WILL GROW TO $6,470.11 AT AGE 21

ADDED DEPOSITS		THREE YEAR GROWTH	TOTAL END OF PERIOD
Ages 3 – 6 (36 months)	$8 monthly ($2 weekly)	$334.34	$434.34
Ages 6 – 9 (36 months)	$12 monthly ($3 weekly)	$557.46	$991.80
Ages 9 – 12 (36 months)	$16 monthly ($4 weekly)	$824.42	$1,816.22
Ages 12 – 15 (36 months)	$20 monthly ($5 weekly)	$1,143.91	$2,960.13
Ages 15 – 18 (36 months)	$24 monthly ($6 weekly)	$1,526.23	$4,486.36
Ages 18 – 21 (36 months)	$28 monthly ($7 weekly)	$1,983.75	$6,470.11

CHOICES

When children first get possession of money, their first inclination will be to spend it and buy something. There are many temptations for children just as there are for adults. One of the most important things parents should teach their children is that they do have *choices* to make about what they do with their money. Many adults get into financial difficulties because they have never learned they do have choices.

A key lesson to pass along to children is that money management is all about *choices*. They can spend all of their money or *"Save* Some, *Spend* Some." They can keep their savings at home or take them to a bank and deposit them in a savings account, where their funds will earn interest. They can choose to spend money as it comes into their possession, or they can put part or all of it away to use to buy something bigger or better at some later date. They can choose to spend it on something disposable that will be consumed or worn out or that may not even be of interest to them a few months or years into the future. Or they can choose to save for something that will give them greater enjoyment in the years ahead.

CHOICES — CHOICES — CHOICES!!

HELPING CHILDREN DETECT "MONEY LEAKS"

Soon after children start receiving a weekly allowance is a good time to introduce them to the system of detecting "money leaks." (It is also recommended for families in a later chapter in this book.)

As soon as the child masters simple arithmetic have him or her keep a record of every *penny* spent and the item purchased for a period of, for example, two weeks. At the end of the period this exercise will make the child aware of the amount of money he or she has spent on various items.

The benefit of this exercise will probably be that the child will be surprised at just where his or her money is really going, often for things not as important as they seemed at the time of purchase. It will be good to repeat this exercise every two or three years as the child becomes older.

"BROKE"

Along the way a child will probably experience the feeling of being "broke." That will be good because it will demonstrate to the child that he or she *needs* a system to keep that from happening again.

Wise parents will use these times as a learning opportunity, resisting the urge to "loan" or give the child money. That will help the child understand the reality of living within his or her income.

MORE ABOUT THE IMPORTANCE OF THE "FOUR-'S' SYSTEM" THROUGH THE YEARS

The message will always be to follow the "Four-'S' System" — Save Some, Spend Some. *"Save* some and *spend* some" each time children receive money or to *save it all,* if possible, any time they receive money.

More money will generally be spent than saved, but the emphasis is placed on *"save."* Keep that priority constantly in mind.

THE EARLY "ALLOWANCE" YEARS

A new era in money management occurs when children start receiving an allowance when they reach grade school or possibly an earlier age.

Parents are encouraged to begin a very important procedure when their children first receive allowances. It might be called a "silent influence" toward money management.

Very simply, the child should be given the weekly allowance on the same day each week and as close as possible to the same hour. This will instill in the mind of the child the importance of having a definite plan rather than having a "hit and miss" allowance system that becomes a "no system." The example of the parents having a system will quietly lead the child into a system.

55

An important part of the timing is to present the allowance early in the week. The child can then be *planning* in advance of the period during the week when most of the spending occurs. Sunday evening is suggested as the time to present the allowance. It is also suggested it be presented in a previously prepared envelope as a symbol of having a system. Presentation of the envelope sometimes by the father and sometimes by the mother would provide an additional message that the parents have a cooperative plan in which both of them participate.

Parents taking money out of a pocket or a purse on different days, and at different times, sets an example for the child to save and spend in the same "no plan" way.

Introducing children to a definite system that continues through the years will benefit the children the rest of their lives. It will become a "way of life."

The routine should become formal with a specific goal of the percentage that should be saved each time money is received.

Additional emphasis can be placed on saving by making the allowance and saving as large as possible for the age of the child.

If the first allowance is $2, it would be well to give it in change and a dollar bill. Give, for example, $1 in change and encourage them to put 50 cents in the piggy bank, which will be taken later to the *big* bank. There will then be $1.50 to spend. The lesson of saving something out of each bit of income will remain forever.

AN ALLOWANCE PLUS PAY FOR SERVICES PERFORMED

The next level of giving children allowances may be the most important training.

At this stage, give the allowance a new meaning by indicating part of the money is pay for work performed around the home to enable the child to make miscellaneous purchases for his or her needs or wishes. If the work is not performed, that amount of the allowance should not be paid. Very importantly, part of this procedure is to teach the child he or she can earn money and start learning to spend it wisely.

If the allowance is $5 per week, the child might be encouraged to save $1 or more. The remaining $4 might be described as "$2 as part of your allowance and $2 as pay for your doing assigned chores around the house." Once again, the payment should be conditioned on "*Save* Some, *Spend* Some."

Every year or so, the allowance and the number of chores to be performed should be increased.

When a child is in the seventh or eighth grade, parents should start another step in the training program. By this time a child can perform more tasks around home for which compensation is paid. The child also can earn money by working for others.

When high school days arrive, the part of the allowance for chores will increase. Each year, the allowances *and* work assignments will be increasing and so should the savings.

At the same time, a child's expenses will be increasing. This marks the time the child needs to *start his or her own money management system.*

The system requires estimates on what the child plans to spend for various types of expenses. It will be timely to decide through the years what percentage of income should be saved. The "Four-'S' System" — *Save Some, Spend Some* — gets more important as the years go by.

The system from there on will follow basically the same formula, but with more income. That means increasing amounts to save and increasing amounts to spend.

When a child reaches the college years, the system should be a way of life. As the child, now an adult, chooses a favorite field of work and gets married, the system will be in place.

If a child has a money management system firmly in place, the parents deserve a great sense of satisfaction for helping the child develop that system. The child should be deeply appreciative of the great start his or her parents have given him or her toward a life of security and happiness.

THE IMPORTANT MONTHLY BALANCING OF A CHECKING ACCOUNT

This is a composite of procedures recommended by all banks.

One of the best ways to control spending and live within your income is to *always* be aware of how much money you have available. The best way to know how much money you have is to have a bank checking account and keep your checkbook records *up-to-the-minute.*

Your checkbook should contain a *check register* in addition to the checks. The check register is a place to record the checks written, deposits made and the up-to-the-minute balance of how much money is in the account. Every time a check is written, the check number, date, name of payee (person, store or company) and the amount of the check should be written in the check register.

Every time a deposit is made, the amount of the deposit, the date and the source of the money also should be written in the check register. *Your balance should be re-calculated with a new total each time a deposit is made, a check is written or another deduction is made.*

A problem many people have is getting in a hurry and forgetting to record a check written or a deposit made. When people forget a transaction, they lose track of their bank balance and easily can end up spending more money than they have in the bank. When this happens, they also will be charged an overdraft fee, which will further reduce their balance.

What people need is a way to *make sure* they have recorded all necessary information and have up-to-the-minute information regarding their bank balance.

At the end of this chapter is a form called *"The Easy Way to Balance Your Checkbook."* Completing this form every month, when you receive your bank statement, will help you be sure you haven't failed to record any transactions during the month. Many banks put a similar form on the back of the bank statement for you to use. It doesn't matter what form you use as long as you record all necessary information.

Let's review the procedure:

Although you may use the checkbook almost every day, you need to confirm your balance once a month when you get your monthly bank statement. You should keep your records up-to-the-minute, but this double check is important.

Since you must rely on the balance in your account, it is very important to keep it up-to-date. Here are a few tips that can help:

When you make deposits, write checks, make ATM or debit card withdrawals, enter them in your check register *immediately.* Don't wait until later. You might forget. You can order checks that make a carbon copy that can be helpful as you re-check your figures.

You may have payments that are *automatically* withdrawn from your bank account. House payments and utility payments are commonly handled as automatic payments. Enter those payments in your check register at the earliest possible date. You may receive a notice in the mail that a payment has been made from your account. If so, enter the amount of the automatic payment in the check register when you receive the notice.

In some cases there might *not* be a notice sent to you. Many check registers have a section in the back to record the amount and time of the month those payments will be deducted from your account. If not, develop your own reminder list.

If you have direct deposit of your compensation, enter the amount of the deposit into your check register when you get confirmation the payment has been made.

A good plan is to calculate your new balance immediately after each transaction is recorded. You may also want to occasionally check your balance, perhaps mid-month, by using automated or online banking services offered by most banks.

Make a habit of following these tips and balancing your bank account each month. This will help you control spending, stay within your money management system and enjoy the peace of mind from knowing your bank account is in accurate condition.

1. ***Bank Balance***
   This is the ending balance
   shown on your bank statement.

2. **Add Any Deposits Shown in
   Your Check Register But Not
   Shown on the Bank Statement**

3. **Subtotal**

4. **Subtract Outstanding Checks**
   These are checks shown in your check
   register but not shown on the bank statement.

Check #	Amount	Check #	Amount

Total Outstanding Checks

5. **Balance**
   This balance should agree with the
   balance in the check register. You will
   first have to record and deduct bank
   service charges (if any) in your
   register and add interest (if any).

If the two balances do not agree, you generally have either a mistake in the math calculations
or have not recorded a transaction. In rare cases
the bank could have made a mistake, which you
will need to call to their attention.

INSURANCE —
THE MAJOR TYPES:
AUTOMOBILE-HOUSEHOLD
LIFE-DISABILITY-HEALTH

GREG SCOTT

Greg Scott is a longtime professional in the field of life and other insurance. He is a Certified Life Underwriter, a Life and Qualifying Member of the Million Dollar Round Table, a recipient of the National Quality Award, a member of the National Association of Insurance and Financial Advisors and a member of the New York Life Executive Council.

WHAT IS INSURANCE?

The dictionary says:

"Protection against loss. A contract guaranteeing compensation to the insured, or a specified party, in the event of a death, disability, fire, or any stated circumstance."

Because there are many types of possible losses, individuals and families need a variety of insurance to protect against such losses. The pressure of living within the family income frequently results in important insurance not being carried. That puts pressure on the family money management system to provide the money for such coverage.

People have to analyze their own needs and protect themselves against losses from some things that might occur and other things, like death, that are certain to occur.

Only a very few people have sufficient money to be self-insurers by setting money aside to cover possible losses. Everyone else needs to pay a company a premium to provide money needed when unpleasant *possibilities* become *realities*.

Insurance in various forms should rate a higher money management priority than it generally receives.

Various types of insurance are a "must" in the financial management of every individual or family.

All states in the United States have an insurance regulatory department. All of them have a wide range of information available free of charge.

While insurance is regulated, all companies don't have the same coverage and rates. Shop around and make sure you are getting the best coverage and rates.

AUTOMOBILE LIABILITY

All states have laws that require automobile owners to have liability insurance. This ensures those who receive physical injuries or property damages will be compensated if the driver was at fault.

It also protects the driver from having to personally pay for physical or property damages received by others. Without insurance, this would be personal money the driver may or may not have. This required insurance might be described as *enforced money management.*

Collision insurance for damages to *your own car or health is not required* and is expensive. You can save money, however, by increasing the deductible on your policy. The deductible is the amount for which you are *personally* responsible, not the insurance company.

The higher the deductible, the lower the premium you will pay. With a deductible, *you in effect become a partial self-insurer. You have to be personally prepared to provide the money to cover that part of the loss if you damage your own car.* The insurance company then will be responsible for the amount in excess of the deductible. Get all of the figures and then make your choices.

You can help yourself get the lowest auto insurance rates by driving carefully and avoiding traffic tickets. Many companies also offer lower auto rates to drivers who complete a defensive driving course.

A clean driving record without any violations also will help you get the lowest possible rates. Many young drivers still in school should also be aware that some companies give a discount on the premium to students who achieve a specified grade point average. *It pays to study!*

HOUSEHOLD

Household insurance generally protects against loss resulting from fire or wind damage to your home. Damage from a flood is generally not covered. You probably will need a separate policy if you fear flood damage.

The usual homeowner's insurance policy also protects against loss or damage to the *contents* of your home. A similar renter's policy is available for people who rent their homes or apartments.

The renter's policy may or may not offer *liability protection* if someone has an accident or injury involving the premises you occupy.

LIFE INSURANCE

First consider the various forms of life insurance. In life insurance — as with all goods and services available for purchase — generally what you get is in line with what you pay.

TERM LIFE INSURANCE

Term life insurance takes fewer dollars but may not be the least expensive of all types of life insurance in the long run. It insures an individual for a set period of time. For example, the policy may expire at the end of a 5-, 10-, 15-, 20- or 30-year period, or a specified time such as age 70 or upon the death of the insured person.

If the insured has the option and wishes to continue the contract past the expiration date, he or she must re-qualify medically prior to that date. If they wait until the end of the term is reached to re-qualify medically, the cost may become high.

Term life builds no cash value, and the premiums will *increase* as the insured ages. Term insurance is frequently used for short-term situations such as guaranteeing that a debt coming due will be satisfied by the proceeds from a life insurance policy if the debtor dies before the debt is paid.

Term insurance is also for individuals who need substantial insurance coverage but do not have funds available at the time for the generally, but temporarily, higher premiums of "whole life" insurance.

68

WHOLE LIFE INSURANCE

Whole life insurance is designed to last an entire lifetime without expiring as term insurance does. This type of coverage builds equity referred to as "cash surrender value" that can be available through a policy loan.

If whole life is purchased from a *mutual* insurance company, the policyowner normally will receive an annual dividend credited to the policy that will help build cash value. With a *stock* insurance company, the dividend, or a portion of the dividend, goes to the stockholders of the insurance company instead of the insured. On the other hand, the cost of premiums also might vary. All companies do not have the same benefits and costs. *The net costs of insurance will vary and have to be carefully calculated and considered.*

Whole life premiums are higher than term insurance initially but less expensive over the life of the policy.

VARIABLE UNIVERSAL LIFE

Variable universal life insurance is a type of life insurance that lets customers invest their cash values in mutual funds under the supervision of the insurance company.

Although variable universal life contracts do not have the same guarantee as whole life contracts, the customer can actively manage the values and hopefully earn a higher return than traditional whole life.

Variable life is becoming more popular as insureds assume a more active role in managing their funds.

SURVIVOR WHOLE LIFE— SECOND TO DIE

Survivor whole life is a contract that is based on the lives of two insureds. This typically drives down the cost of the policy because the death benefit is not paid until the time of the second death.

This type of insurance is normally used in estate planning or in more specialized situations.

DISABILITY INCOME INSURANCE

Disability income insurance should be a "must" for workers in high risk of injury types of work and is very desirable for others.

This replaces the lost income for insureds who become disabled and unable to work. Some contracts pay a prorated amount even if the insured returns to work part-time.

Premiums will remain constant with a non-cancellable type of policy. Other policies provide for a guaranteed renewable contract on which the issuing company may change premiums.

If a man had a cash machine that automatically distributed his daily earnings each day at 5 p.m., he very likely would consider insuring the machine against breakdown. That illustrates the need for disability income insurance.

The need for this insurance varies according to the risks of physical impairment in various industries. Premiums also vary accordingly. The safest course for a worker is to have some disability insurance compared to other needs and benefits for the family.

Disability insurance is important in providing financial security. If a wage earner becomes ill or injured, income will be needed to sustain the family. Disability insurance is the best way to do so if there are no other funds to enable the family to carry on.

The cost of disability insurance is based on a combination of the ages of the insured persons, their annual incomes and the risks in their type of work.

Some examples are on the following chart. Persons who become disabled receive approximately two-thirds of their annual income. Income from the benefits is subject to income taxes for the employee if the employer pays the premium.

Following is a chart indicating the costs of disability insurance.

EXAMPLES OF THE COSTS OF DISABILITY INSURANCE			
Age at the time the policy is purchased	Annual Income	Monthly Premiums	Annual Benefit
25	$15,000	$24	$9,000
30	$20,000	$33	$13,333
40	$30,000	$73	$20,000
50	$40,000	$155	$26,667

HEALTH

There are as many types and features in health insurance as there are colors in a rainbow.

Often people believe they and their family members have good health and therefore do not need insurance. However, statistics indicate otherwise.

Study all of the forms of health insurance available to you. Consider some level of coverage a "must" for you and your family. Without health insurance, your family money management system could be completely wrecked in a matter of a few days.

Because health insurance is expensive, there is a big temptation to feel you don't need it and try to get by without it. If you feel you *might not* be able to pay for insurance for routine medical expenses, at least protect yourselves against expenses of a *major illness or accident.*

Many employers offer some form of health insurance through a company group plan. Group plans are usually less expensive than individual health insurance. Be sure to take advantage of any group plans for which you qualify. These might include your own company, veterans' organizations, fraternal groups, clubs and business cooperatives.

If you do not qualify for any group plan, check the individual plans thoroughly. There are many policies on the market that vary in the type of coverage they offer. If you cannot afford full coverage, protect yourself and your family by purchasing what you can afford.

Families with young children who meet income eligibility guidelines may qualify for insurance for the children at a greatly reduced rate through special federal government and private programs.

If you have problems obtaining health insurance coverage because of a pre-existing condition, check with the insurance department in your state. They probably can give you information that will be helpful.

People do get sick, injured and disabled, and do experience home and auto damages. Insurance should be a top priority in your money management planning.

Talk to two or three insurance sales representatives for each type of insurance and ask them what they have to offer. Then look to the representative you feel is best qualified and has the best coverage for you. Study this subject carefully and choose what is best for you and your family.

Many premiums can be payable monthly for your convenience in keeping your records. If the premium has to be paid annually or semi-annually, you will need to set that money aside each month so it is available when the premiums become due.

EXAMPLES OF THE COSTS OF LIFE AND DISABILITY INSURANCE

This information will be helpful later as you develop your maximum spending goals in your money management planning. There will be expense categories for insurance, and you will need to know the costs of life and disability and other types of insurance you may not be buying at this time.

The preceding chapter has hopefully demonstrated the importance of having life and disability insurance. The purpose of this chapter is to give you some figures on the benefits and costs of such insurance.

In the preceding chapter, whole life insurance and term life insurance were described. The cost of insurance for both men and women is based on their life expectancies. This involves the ages of the insured persons at the time the policy is purchased and the expected number of years they will live.

The cost of life insurance for a woman is approximately the same as insurance on a man. The following chart uses the same examples of monthly and annual costs for a non-smoking man or woman for ages from 25 to 50 years — with amounts of coverage from $25,000 to $100,000.

COSTS OF PREMIUMS FOR WHOLE LIFE INSURANCE BASED ON AGE AND AMOUNT OF COVERAGE

Age	$50,000		$75,000		$100,000	
	Monthly	Annual	Monthly	Annual	Monthly	Annual
25	$38.00	$426.50	$54.50	$614.75	$69.00	$782.00
30	$46.00	$517.00	$66.50	$750.50	$85.00	$956.00
35	$57.50	$647.50	$83.75	$946.25	$107.00	$1,208.00
40	$71.50	$801.50	$104.75	$1,177.25	$133.00	$1,500.00
50	$118.00	$1,334.50	$174.50	$1,976.75	$222.00	$2,513.00

Next is a similar chart on the costs of term life insurance.

COSTS OF PREMIUMS FOR TERM LIFE INSURANCE BASED ON AGE AND AMOUNT OF COVERAGE

Age	$50,000		$75,000		$100,000	
	Monthly	Annual	Monthly	Annual	Monthly	Annual
25	$9.05	$96.00	$11.08	$119.00	$13.10	$142.00
30	$9.20	$97.50	$11.30	$121.25	$13.40	$145.00
35	$9.55	$101.50	$11.83	$127.25	$14.10	$153.00
40	$11.15	$120.00	$14.23	$155.00	$17.30	$190.00
50	$18.85	$207.50	$25.78	$286.25	$32.70	$365.00

Note that for a few dollars per month in additional cost you can get much higher protection.

Wouldn't those extra coverage dollars be a great comfort to you and your family?

Disability insurance is particularly important in some industries. If a wage earner becomes ill or injured, income will be needed to sustain the family. Disability insurance is the best choice if there are no other funds to enable the family to carry on.

The cost of disability insurance is based on a combination of the age of the insured person and his or her annual income. The following chart shows some examples of the rates. Persons who become disabled will generally receive approximately two-thirds of their annual incomes.

COSTS AND BENEFITS OF DISABILITY INSURANCE BASED ON AGE AND AMOUNT OF COVERAGE		
Age at the time the policy is purchased	Coverage/ Monthly Benefit	Monthly Premium
25	$1,250	$ 23.47
30	$1,666	$ 34.57
40	$2,500	$ 75.73
50	$4,000	$ 155.39

A very important point! Study the various types and costs of insurance you will need so you will have your figures ready later when you develop your maximum expense goals for the insurance category. Insurance presents many complex issues. If you have any questions we suggest you confer with your accountant, financial or estate planner.

BUILDING FAMILY SECURITY — HOW MONEY "GROWS"

Professional financial counselors have long advocated "pay yourself first" as the first step in family security. Begin with setting aside a planned amount each month in a savings account that earns a specified percent of interest. The benefits that will result from such a long-term plan are generally very underestimated.

Dollars placed in an investment account like a savings account, U.S. government bonds and Series EE bonds available at banks, 401(k) plans, mutual funds, etc., each month will grow into a significant amount in a few years. Following is another chart that demonstrates that money will grow.

A CHART SHOWING HOW MONEY GROWS					
IF THIS AMOUNT IS DEPOSITED IN A SAVINGS ACCOUNT EACH MONTH	WITH 6% INTEREST COMPOUNDED MONTHLY THE PRINCIPAL AND INTEREST WILL GROW TO THESE AMOUNTS IN THE YEARS INDICATED				
	10 Years	20 Years	30 Years	40 Years	50 Years
$ 10	$1,639	$4,620	$10,045	$19,915	$37,872
$ 25	$4,097	$11,551	$25,113	$49,787	$94,680
$ 50	$8,194	$23,102	$50,226	$99,574	$189,360
$100	$16,388	$46,204	$100,452	$199,148	$378,720
$200	$32,776	$92,408	$200,904	$398,296	$757,440

MASTERING THE CHALLENGES OF "KEEPING UP WITH THE JONESES"

MARION O'BRIEN, PH.D.

Dr. O'Brien received her bachelor's degree from Gettysburg College, Gettysburg, Pa., her master's in human development and her doctorate in developmental and child psychology from The University of Kansas. She became a member of the faculty of the university in 1983 and served as a professor in the Department of Human Development and Family Life. In 2001 she joined the faculty of the University of North Carolina as professor in the Department of Human Development and Family Studies.

Dr. O'Brien's areas of scientific interest have included parental attitudes, parenting behavior, children's social-emotional development and child care and its effects on children and families.

Dr. O'Brien has been the recipient of many grants for research. She is the author of four books and more than 40 journal articles in her field.

Dr. O'Brien is married to John O'Brien, Ph.D., and he has also joined the faculty of the University of North Carolina in his field as a professor of biology.

The expression "Keeping Up With the Joneses" started in New York in 1913 when an artist by the name of Arthur Momand and his wife realized they were overspending their income in an effort to keep up with the tastes and incomes of some of their neighbors in an upscale neighborhood.

After realizing their mistakes, they decided to move down to a lifestyle they could afford. He decided to capitalize on their experience and started a comic strip poking fun at the trials and tribulations of others who were doing the same unwise things he and his wife had been doing.

He called the comic strip "Keeping Up With the Joneses." It ran for 28 years in newspapers all over the country. Now, 60 years later, we don't have the artist's reminders, but we have some general and specific thoughts for your consideration.

PARENTS NEED TO LEAD

The first step in facing the challenges of "Keeping Up With the Joneses," (hereafter referred to for brevity as KUWTJ), starts with the parents *mastering* those challenges.

The following statement presents an ultimate goal for all members of the family to accept.

We Are A Happy Family

In our family we have more of the things of life money will buy than some families have. We have less of the things of life money will buy than some families have.

We are a happy family even though there are some things we cannot afford. Having less money than some other families does not keep us from being a happy family.

The important thing is that we be happy and not worry about others having more to spend than we have.

It was planned that the previous statement would be on one page and be easily copied. We hope every family will have a copy made and post it on the refrigerator door for all to read and consider. Perhaps more importantly, it should be talked about enough times for all members of the family to fully understand it.

Children will learn this message not only from what parents say but also from how parents act. Fathers and mothers who show jealousy or envy of what others have will teach their children to feel the same way. Parents who enjoy what they *do* have and express satisfaction with their own lives will have children who also will be content.

WATCHING YOUR OWN SPENDING

A point of beginning for parents is to review some of their own past purchases. It is easy for you to discover if *you* suffer from KUWTJ thinking.

Just take an inventory of the last 6 to 10 purchases you made that were in the non-essential category. Ask yourselves why you bought those items. Answer honestly. Do you even wear the clothes you bought because they were similar to those of a friend? How often do you use that electronic item you "had to have?" Can you afford the investment and expenses of your luxury car?

Consider how much you truly value each of those purchases. If they are not clearly important to you, then you may have been struck by the "Keeping Up With the Joneses" thinking.

Many people overspend and have difficulties mastering personal and family money management because of the challenges of "Keeping Up With the Joneses." If parents are caught up in competition over who can buy the most, they must anticipate their children will follow their lead. Parents who meet the KUWTJ challenges teach their children positive attitudes about money and spending.

DECIDING TO BUY OR NOT

When tempted to KUWTJ, stop and think. Do not assume that just because friends or neighbors have purchased something is a sign they can afford it. Perhaps they were influenced by others to buy something *they* could not afford. Or perhaps they, too, are trying to KUWTJ, possibly even trying to keep up with you!

Basing your purchases on what *someone else* buys or owns can cause many financial problems. Don't let it happen to you!

As you make a decision to purchase something, always ask yourself why you are buying the item. Is this something you really need or even want, or are you making the purchase merely to feel good at the moment?

Generally, we do not want to be different from our friends and neighbors. There will always be things that others own that we cannot afford. All our lives we are called upon to make sensible choices. By making good choices yourself, you also help your child learn to make good choices. Recognizing this can help you avoid unwise purchases in the future.

GUIDING YOUR CHILDREN

You should talk with your children about the temptations *you* feel to buy things, and why you choose *not* to buy everything that looks appealing to you. This will help them learn to think through their own purchases ahead of time, rather than making impulsive decisions. When *you* model making *good* choices, you help your child learn to make *good* choices too.

CHILDREN ARE BOMBARDED!

Today's children are bombarded with messages to buy things. Each day, children see and hear thousands of advertising messages. Hundreds of these are geared specifically to youngsters. It is no wonder children want the things they hear about so glowingly on TV, see displayed so attractively in store windows or are items that their friends have.

The challenge for parents is to help children discriminate — between things that are worthwhile and things that are not — between quality toys and junk — between their real needs and desires and their passing fancies.

The *way parents respond to children's requests* — whether for toys, sports equipment or trendy clothing — communicates a lot to children.

An angry response to a child's request often will be perceived by a child as a selfish desire on the parent's part not to spend money on the child. This will be the child's feeling even when the parent's actual intent was to protect the child from wasting money or being disappointed.

A belittling or critical response — "I can't believe you want one of those!" or "Those are no good" — may be seen by a child as personal rejection of the child, not as an objective evaluation of the child's request.

How, then, can parents respond to children when they ask to buy things that are inappropriate, too expensive or of poor quality?

WHEN CHILDREN ARE YOUNG

For children who are in the early school years, wishes and desires often come and go quickly. Parents do best to maintain a sense of proportion — *and* a sense of humor. Following are some suggestions for how parents can handle children's requests.

ACKNOWLEDGE YOUR CHILD'S DESIRES

Even if you think what your child is wishing for is totally unrealistic and unnecessary — such as the fifteenth computer game with *Star* in the title — at the moment this wish is important to your child. It is best to *avoid an immediate negative reaction* and instead give yourself a minute to think *how your child feels*. Then you will be able to acknowledge, aloud, that his feeling is real and important to him and therefore important to you, too.

This does not mean that you are required to buy what your child wants right at the time your child wants it. Instead, use techniques to help your child learn that *everyone* wants more things than they can afford.

PLAY A WISHING GAME WITH YOUR CHILD

Even as mature and responsible adults, we often want things that do not really make sense for us to buy. And certainly we can think about things that would be fun to have or do that are absolutely impossible! When children express wishes, we can share this experience with them in a playful and funny way.

For example, if you are in the car with your 10-year-old daughter and she suddenly says, "I just have to have a new pair of Doc Martens. These are last year's style!" Your first reaction is probably going to be something like, "You can't be serious! I paid $120 for those shoes not 6 months ago!" Instead of challenging her in this way, you can indulge her fantasy to have every new item of clothing that any of her friends are wearing — by sharing your own wishes.

Rather than responding with anger or annoyance, you can say, "That *would* be nice! Let's think about all the clothes we'd like to have. I've *always* wanted an evening gown that was covered with sequins. How about you?" Usually, by encouraging your child to express her wishes and by adding in some of yours that are clearly not realistic, the conversation will become silly and fun, and the impracticality of the original request will be obvious.

ENCOURAGE YOUR CHILD TO SAVE

When you give your children an allowance or they receive occasional monetary gifts from relatives, they have a small source of money to save for things they really want. It is important, however, for parents to help guide children's savings goals in a realistic way. Most young children cannot plan beyond a period of a few weeks. Therefore, encouraging your children to save for a *big* item they would not be able to purchase for months is likely to be frustrating rather than rewarding. Gradually building a bank savings account falls in a different category.

Setting up a very short-term savings plan — perhaps combined with some additional chores and certainly with some no-strings-attached financial help from you — that will allow children to buy something they want within 2 or 3 weeks, is a good way to demonstrate to them the benefits of saving.

IN THE TEEN YEARS

Dealing with teenagers' wishes and desires requires even more restraint and thoughtfulness by the parents. Teens do a lot of testing of parents' limits, and their judgment about money and the value of the things they want are usually not the best. To avoid confrontation and conflict over money and purchases, parents need to *plan ahead*.

If you sense a child is building too big a dream for the future, you can start building a counter idea in advance before it becomes apparent you are doing so.

BE CLEAR ABOUT MONEY ISSUES

It is important for parents to set explicit rules or standards in all areas, and money is included here. Talk with your teen about money. Specify how much allowance you feel is appropriate. If you expect your teenager to earn money on his or her own, say so.

Make a list of what you expect your teenager to buy with their allowance or their earnings from their after-school jobs. Also list what they can expect you to buy for them. Avoid dealing with money issues one at a time but instead make an agreement that covers a set period of time.

Parents also must realize that any such agreement can last only a few months or so and should then be re-examined and re-negotiated. You or your teen might be unhappy with the way the agreement has worked. If so, you must work together in a cooperative way to work out a new plan. Staying open to changes in the level of maturity of your teen is one of the biggest challenges of being a parent in these years.

LET YOUR TEEN WASTE MONEY SOMETIMES

Like most of us, teens truly learn from experience. It is unfortunate that they cannot really learn from our experience but must make their own mistakes. And it is very hard for parents to watch what they know are mistakes.

If your teenager is spending his or her own money — either allowance money or earned money — you really have less to say about what they purchase. Some teens will accept soft coaching, but others resist even this. Learn to keep your strong opinions to yourself. And never, ever, show signs of pleasure if your child's unwise purchase turns out to be a real disappointment.

When you provide money for your teens — to buy clothes, for example — let them know ahead of time the total amount they can spend. Ask them to tell you what clothes they think they need. Recommend that they plan a budget for spending the total.

Most teens will not want to follow your advice. But your job is to stick to your agreed-upon total, letting them make the decisions about the individual items they purchase. You can expect, at least the first time you do this, that your teen will buy an expensive pair of jeans and have little left over for the other needed items. This is called experience.

INCLUDE YOUR TEEN
IN FAMILY DECISIONS

Learning to handle money and make decisions about how it is spent is a big task. Teens often do not realize that adults also have to make hard decisions and go without things they really want. Make your teenagers part of your family discussions about purchases, trips or just making ends meet. Give them experience with thinking through the complicated issues that every family faces in matching expenses to income.

It also can be helpful for teenagers to be aware of the everyday costs of living. Having a family budget and letting teens see it can help make them more knowledgeable about the costs of maintaining a household. Although teens may not seem very interested in your budget, the knowledge they gain from your open and honest communication about money will help them make better personal decisions in the long run.

The most important gift parents can give their children is a feeling of love, security and confidence. No amount of money can buy those gifts.

91

THE FUNDAMENTALS OF STOCK MARKET INVESTING

AL WILLIAMS JR.

Al Williams Jr. has been a financial consultant in Topeka, Kansas, for 24 years. He is a vice-president of Fahnestock & Co., Inc., members of the New York Stock Exchange and other principal exchanges. He has a bachelor of arts degree in business administration from Vanderbilt University. He is a past member of The American Funds President's Club, the Franklin Templeton Kite and Key Club, and an Executive Board Member of the Nuveen Advisory Council. In 1997, he won the Stock Contest based on Profitability in Purchasing and Selling Securities sponsored by The Topeka Capital-Journal.

Interest in the stock and bond market or other investments usually occurs after a savings account has been solidly established.

There comes a time when a higher return on the money is desired and attention is turned to investments. At this point people want to start thinking of themselves as investors.

This is where a financial consultant, often called a stockbroker, comes in. These individuals give counsel and advice to help investors decide what stocks and bonds are best for them. The stockbroker then handles the details of purchasing and selling the securities.

The first step to intelligent investing is determining one's investment objectives, such as long-term growth, preservation of assets, generation of income or a combination of several factors.

A stockbroker will help evaluate an investor's tolerance for risk. Normally, potential for possible gain is accompanied by risk of possible loss. Everyone says they want to make money. The key question, however, that each investor must answer is, "How much money can I prudently afford to lose?" A generally strong market makes it difficult for investors to think there is any risk.

Some years ago a broker had a prospective client who was thinking of starting an investment account. The broker asked the client about his tolerance for risk. The client replied that he didn't mind taking risk as long as he didn't lose any money. Unfortunately, things don't work that way.

People who want income from investments are sometimes advised to invest in bonds. Bonds are debt instruments (formal evidence of debt). When you buy a bond, you are lending the issuer of that bond your money. Bonds will pay you interest on a regular basis, plus the return of your money at a set maturity date. An investor may choose a corporate bond because the interest received is higher than interest on a bank savings account or certificate of deposit.

If a person is in a high tax bracket, a tax-free bond offered by a state or city may be more attractive. There are no federal income taxes on the interest from these bonds. In some states, the interest is also tax-free from state income taxes if the bond is a municipal bond issued by that state or an entity within that state.

When you buy stock, also referred to as "equity," you are buying ownership in the company. If the company prospers and increases its earnings, the value of your stock should increase. Historically, buying stocks in well-managed companies in growing industries and holding these stocks for several years produces the best results. Some, but not all, speculative stocks also have done well.

The market has always been volatile. It is generally safer to ignore the volatility and select a long-term strategy as the best chance for successful results.

An example tells a story. An investor bought shares through a stockbroker many years ago in a company with a good reputation. The company and the stock have done well, based on good earnings and several stock splits. A split occurs when a company issues one or more additional shares of stock to stockholders for each share owned. The *total* value of the stock tends to increase after a stock split. The combination of all of these factors has produced an excellent result with a value many times the initial investment.

How do you find good stocks? One of the best ways is to observe what is happening in the company you work for, if it is a publicly traded company, or in other companies that you know something about. Companies that are leaders in their field or have products or processes that are protected by patents are a good place to start.

Watching what people are buying, particularly young people, may point you to the companies that will perform well in the future. It comes down to careful observation, good research and common sense.

A stockbroker and the company's stockholder reports will have useful information. You can do further research by using your public library, the Internet and various reports from newspapers and trade journals.

Once you find a company in which you want to invest, a stockbroker then can place your order. After you become a stockholder, you need to be patient but constantly follow all information about the company.

If the company does well, you may want to buy more stock. If it experiences significant problems, or if the economy turns downward, you may be best served by selling the stock and looking for a new investment. Your stockbroker should be able to help advise you on these decisions.

This analysis barely scratches the surface of investing. Hopefully some of these ideas will stimulate your interest to study further. With the rapid pace of communication, investors never have had more information available. Young people are getting exposed to investing at much earlier ages than they were just a few years ago. The Internet has brought a whole new dimension to investing, most particularly to stock trading. This phenomenon is so much in its infancy that few can visualize how far-reaching its effects may be.

Do your homework, study hard, be patient, continue to study the stocks you buy and you will find fascination, fun and success with your investments.

PART III
EXAMPLES OF OPPORTUNITIES
TO CONTROL EXPENSES —
HELP IN MAKING DECISIONS

PART III
EXAMPLES OF OPPORTUNITIES
TO CONTROL EXPENSES —
HELP IN MAKING DECISIONS

There is an old expression: "A problem well analyzed is more than half solved." That fits the development of a money management system.

Why do you feel you need a money management system? How big or small are your problems?

Your desire to have a money management system is probably based on the fact your expenses tend to be higher than your income or that you want to do some planning that will present that situation from developing.

You will be establishing goals for the amounts of money you plan to spend on various subjects and it is important you know how big are the challenges you face. Every individual or family needs to establish guidelines so they can meet their goals. Know how big a challenge you face, and plan your spending accordingly.

Keep in mind that if your expenses are running too high, the remedy will probably lie in cutting a number of expenses slightly rather than cutting two or three expenses a lot.

With that background, consider the money-saving suggestions in the following chapters.

DETECTING "MONEY LEAKS"

Benjamin Franklin was previously quoted as saying, "Beware of little expenses. A small leak will sink a great ship."

Every household has "money leaks" of which no one in the family is sufficiently aware. These money leaks might be likened to an efficiency leak in a heating or cooling system. It is hard to detect, but in time can be expensive.

Some money leaks in families are also hard to detect. One small leak might go unnoticed. When increases in the number and size of leaks occur, the subject gets attention. The chapters in Part I are designed to help you identify possible money leaks in your household.

The most likely money leaks will result from the cash you carry in your pocket or purse, so carry as little cash as possible. To stop payday money leaks, don't get your paycheck cashed and start spending it on your way home. Deposit your paycheck in a bank account and then spend from it.

You may deposit your checks or you may authorize your employers to make direct deposits to your bank or banks.

Write checks for most things other than your daily cash requirements. The leaks will be less likely to occur when you write checks.

Work hard at developing the attitude that *if you can afford something, you can afford it just as much the day before payday as on payday or later.*

Following is a system used by many to help detect some of those leaks. Every member of the family is given a small pocket-sized notebook. For a period of two weeks, everyone in the family writes down each day all of the items and amounts, down to the penny, for which they spend money.

They are urged to be particularly mindful of the amounts they spend for soft drinks, fast food, miscellaneous school expenses, movie rentals, gasoline, hair care, fun, cigarettes, etc.

The figures for one day won't seem significant. Most family members will be surprised, however, when the figures are totaled after two weeks and they learn how many soft drinks they have been sipping — how many hamburgers they have been eating — how much gasoline they have been buying — how many cigarettes they have been smoking — and on and on.

Turn their amazement into a plus by getting all family members to agree they will eliminate or greatly reduce all non-essential spending.

This is a great family exercise. Try it, and you will benefit from it. One family felt it was so educational and beneficial they continued it for three months. They discovered and eliminated additional money leaks they hadn't detected in the first two weeks.

Start your family money leaks survey at this time so you will have current information when you later establish your maximum spending goals in your many categories of expenses.

THE ULTIMATE TEST — WHAT CAN WE AFFORD?

WHAT CAN WE AFFORD? For proper emphasis on each of those four words, the question needs to be repeated four times with the emphasis moving to each word. READ IT ALOUD!!

<u>WHAT</u> CAN WE AFFORD?
WHAT <u>CAN</u> WE AFFORD?
WHAT CAN <u>WE</u> AFFORD?
WHAT CAN WE <u>AFFORD</u>?

People like to dream about what they can afford or would like to be able to afford. Sooner or later, everyone has to face the realities. The earlier people face those realities, the better off and happier they will be. The longer they fail to face the realities, the more they will suffer in family difficulties, employment performance and lack of happiness.

Difficulties breed unhappiness, and one of the greatest difficulties people face is living within their income, at whatever their income level might be.

The world is full of people who are sustained by the barest necessities of life and yet are happier than many people who have an abundance of money and material things. *Success and wealth should be measured in happiness and contentment rather than in dollars.*

The hard fact of life people must face is that if they can't afford something, they just have to do without it. The fact that people have money in their hands or available through credit or otherwise, doesn't mean they can afford something. *Deciding what can be afforded is the key to family financial planning and is highly rewarding!*

MAGIC WORDS

There are some words that will work like magic in helping solve your money management problems. Those words are — *"We can't afford that."*

Say those words in two situations. First, say them when establishing your maximum spending goals by acknowledging quietly to yourselves, *"We can't afford that."*

You also will need those words *after* you complete your maximum spending goals. Sooner or later, someone or a group will ask you to join them in an event you can't afford or suggest you buy something that is too expensive for you.

That or a similar situation will present a more difficult time for you to say to members of your family, friends, neighbors or business associates, *"We can't afford that."*

You can soften your statement by saying, "We have a *Money Management System* with Maximum Spending Goals, and *we haven't allocated any money for that expense."*

It will be easier for you if you practice in advance the words to be used under those circumstances. Don't be caught off guard! You are not telling others what they should do. You are only speaking softly for yourselves.

It might hurt at the moment to say those words, but the pleasure and self-satisfaction in the future will far outweigh the seeming difficulty of the moment. *Don't apologize for having the courage to do what you know is best for you.* Those around you will admire and respect you for recognizing the realities and may be encouraged to follow your wise and courageous policy.

HOUSING

Many people are living in homes they can't afford because they yielded to the pressure of "Keeping up with the Joneses." When you choose an *affordable* home, your friends will respect you for living within your means and you will be happier.

There is a big temptation to buy a home rather than renting a house or an apartment. People like to feel they are building equity in a house when they make a payment on a home mortgage. They are, but it is a *very slow and very expensive* process.

If ownership and renting of houses were good investments, there would be many houses *for rent.* The fact is, investors have difficulty owning houses, renting them and getting a reasonable return on their investment. From a purely monetary standpoint *most people would be dollars ahead to rent a house or an apartment.*

With so few rental houses available, it frequently seems the only way to get a house that meets your specifications is to buy or build one. If you think of *renting*, know how much rent you can afford. That figure might very well be a guiding figure in making a house payment you can afford.

If you choose to *own your own home, consider all of the costs of ownership* when deciding what you can afford. *Thoroughly* know all of the facts involved! Get a housing or credit counselor to help you! Pre-purchasing counseling is available through the nonprofit Consumer Credit Counseling Service Network. They have offices throughout the United States. Phone (800) 388-2227 for the location of their nearest office. They also can be contacted on the Internet at http://www.nfcc.org.

Many years ago someone defined a boat as "a hole in the water surrounded by a hull into which owners pour money." Those words too frequently also define buying a home. It is also much like buying a car with interest payments that make the total cost *much greater* than a purchase for cash would have been.

Know the answer to the question: *How much will that new home really cost?*

The "American Dream" of owning a new home is one of the toughest financial decisions to make. On the following pages are some examples of the total costs of homes with 15- and 30-year mortgages at 8.25 percent interest.

Home mortgages can be secured for any agreed on number of years with 15- and 30-year periods most frequently used. The 30-year mortgage gives you more time but also results in much more interest being paid.

We first present Chart No. 1 with the figures on the total cost of a 15-year mortgage on homes that would cost between $50,000 and $400,000 if purchased for cash.

CHART NO. 1
COST OF A HOME FINANCED BY A 15-YEAR MORTGAGE AT 8.25% INTEREST AFTER TAKING AN INCOME TAX DEDUCTION ON THE INTEREST PAID

INITIAL COST	INTEREST PAID	ESTIMATE OF TAX DEDUCTION*	NET TOTAL COST	NO. OF PAYMENTS
$50,000	$37,313	($7,463) 20%	$79,850	180
$100,000	$74,625	($18,656) 25%	$155,969	180
$200,000	$149,250	($44,775) 30%	$304,475	180
$300,000	$223,876	($78,357) 35%	$445,519	180
$400,000	$298,500	($119,400) 40%	$579,100	180

*INCOME TAX RATES ON THIS CHART AND THE FOLLOWING THREE CHARTS HAVE BEEN ESTIMATED BASED UPON THE PRESUMED INCOME OF INDIVIDUALS BUYING THE VARIOUS PRICED HOMES

We next present Chart No. 2 with figures on similar priced homes with a 30-year mortgage.

CHART NO. 2
COST OF A HOME FINANCED BY A 30-YEAR MORTGAGE AT 8.25% INTEREST AFTER TAKING AN INCOME TAX DEDUCTION ON THE INTEREST PAID

INITIAL COST	INTEREST PAID	ESTIMATE OF TAX DEDUCTION*	NET TOTAL COST	NO. OF PAYMENTS
$50,000	$85,227	($17,045) 20%	$118,182	360
$100,000	$170,457	($42,614) 25%	$227,843	360
$200,000	$340,911	($102,273) 30%	$438,638	360
$300,000	$511,368	($178,979) 35%	$632,389	360
$400,000	$681,825	($272,730) 40%	$809,095	360

*INCOME TAX RATES ON THIS CHART AND THE FOLLOWING THREE CHARTS HAVE BEEN ESTIMATED BASED UPON THE PRESUMED INCOME OF INDIVIDUALS BUYING THE VARIOUS PRICED HOMES

Yes — $227,843 for a $100,000 house!

When comparing a 15-year mortgage to a 30-year mortgage on Chart No. 1 and Chart No. 2, it is almost shocking to see the difference in total cost of homes that would have the same cash cost.

For example, a $100,000 home costs $95,832 more in total payments with financing over 30 years compared to 15 years. The net total cost is $71,874 higher with a 30-year mortgage even after considering the tax effect of deducting the higher interest amount.

If you can afford a larger monthly payment, you would save a huge amount of interest expense.

The following Chart No. 3 presents figures based on paying an additional $100 each month on the loan.

CHART NO. 3
THIS CHART PRESENTS THE FIGURES ON THE COST OF THE SAME HOUSE IN CHART NO. 1 IF AN ADDITIONAL PAYMENT OF $100 IS MADE EACH MONTH.

INITIAL COST	INTEREST PAID	ESTIMATE OF TAX DEDUCTION*	NET TOTAL COST	NO. OF PAYMENTS
$50,000	$39,048	($7,810) 20%	$81,238	188
$100,000	$104,792	($26,198) 25%	$178,594	241
$200,000	$256,577	($76,973) 30%	$379,604	285
$300,000	$417,818	($146,236) 35%	$571,582	305
$400,000	$582,750	($233,100) 40%	$749,650	317
*INCOME TAX RATES ON THIS CHART AND THE FOLLOWING THREE CHARTS HAVE BEEN ESTIMATED BASED UPON THE PRESUMED INCOME OF INDIVIDUALS BUYING THE VARIOUS PRICED HOMES				

If a buyer decides to pay an additional $250 or $500 each month, the cost of the house will be reduced as indicated on the following charts.

CHART NO. 4
THIS CHART PRESENTS THE FIGURES ON THE COST OF THE SAME HOUSE IN CHART NO. 1 IF AN ADDITIONAL PAYMENT OF $250 IS MADE EACH MONTH.

INITIAL COST	INTEREST PAID	ESTIMATE OF TAX DEDUCTION*	NET TOTAL COST	NO. OF PAYMENTS
$50,000	$22,802	($4,560) 20%	$68,242	117
$100,000	$69,576	($17,394) 25%	$152,182	170
$200,000	$192,678	($57,803) 30%	$334,875	225
$300,000	$334,347	($117,021) 35%	$517,326	254
$400,000	$485,223	($194,089) 40%	$691,134	272

*INCOME TAX RATES ON THIS CHART AND THE FOLLOWING THREE CHARTS HAVE BEEN ESTIMATED BASED UPON THE PRESUMED INCOME OF INDIVIDUALS BUYING THE VARIOUS PRICED HOMES

CHART NO. 5
THIS CHART PRESENTS THE FIGURES ON THE COST OF THE SAME HOUSE IN CHART NO. 1 IF AN ADDITIONAL PAYMENT OF $500 IS MADE EACH MONTH.

INITIAL COST	INTEREST PAID	ESTIMATE OF TAX DEDUCTION*	NET TOTAL COST	NO. OF PAYMENTS
$50,000	$13,713	($2,743) 20%	$60,970	73
$100,000	$45,604	($11,401) 25%	$134,203	117
$200,000	$139,153	($41,746) 30%	$297,407	170
$300,000	$255,532	($89,436) 35%	$466,096	202
$400,000	$385,354	($154,142) 40%	$631,212	225

*INCOME TAX RATES ON THIS CHART AND THE FOLLOWING THREE CHARTS HAVE BEEN ESTIMATED BASED UPON THE PRESUMED INCOME OF INDIVIDUALS BUYING THE VARIOUS PRICED HOMES

111

The decision to accelerate debt payments should include the consideration of a family's total debts.

If you have several different kinds of debts (home mortgage, car loans, credit cards, etc.), you will probably want to first pay off the debts with the highest interest rate. You should also read your loan agreement to determine if you will be charged a penalty for paying off the loan early.

As indicated, the interest on most loans secured by your residence is deductible on your personal income tax returns. That raises the question of what priority should be given to reducing the various debts. If you have a home mortgage and other debts, it would be well to seek the counsel of your tax preparer to determine which debts should receive priority payments.

There are differing opinions on whether to accelerate your mortgage payments in an attempt to pay off your debt sooner, thus reducing the total amount of interest that you pay over the life of the loan. Many financial analysts argue that you are better off to pay only your required mortgage payment and place any extra money that you may have into an investment (mutual funds, bonds, etc.). This concept is driven by the fact that the interest on your residence is generally deductible for income tax purposes and thus reduces the actual effective rate that you are paying on your mortgage.

In reality, everybody will need to look at his or her specific situation (tax brackets, assumed investment rate, willingness to take risks on investments and personal goals). Some individuals may feel more comfortable paying off their mortgage earlier in their lives and thus not worrying about whether they will have the ability to make payments as they get older. Some individuals may not be comfortable investing in the sometimes-volatile stock market, which may provide a nice return, but also may endure periods of high loss.

We have already demonstrated in Charts No. 2 through No. 5 the effects of paying off your mortgage on an accelerated payment scale. For example, Chart No. 2 reflects that the net total cost of a 30-year mortgage on a $200,000 loan is $438,638 after taxes. Chart No. 3 demonstrates that the same loan has a net cost of $379,604 if you can manage to pay an additional $100 dollars per month.

The following chart demonstrates what happens if you pay your mortgage off over the 30-year payment scale and place $100 per month in an investment earning 6 percent or 10 percent instead of paying down your mortgage faster.

FIXED PAYMENT OVER 30 YEARS WITH ADDITIONAL $100 PLACED IN AN INVESTMENT

	6% INVESTMENT	10% INVESTMENT
Principal paid	$200,000	$200,000
Interest paid	$340,911	$340,911
Tax deduction (assumed 30%)	-$102,273	-$102,273
Net payments after tax (See Chart No. 1)	$438,638	$438,638
Deposit of extra $100 per month in investment	$ 36,000	$ 36,000
Additional tax to be paid due to earnings on investment (assumed 30%)	$ 19,486	$ 68,380
Total investment balance at the end of 30 years (6% return)	-$100,954	-$227,933
Net total cost	$393,170	$315,085

As demonstrated, the concept of investing $100 a month in a 6 percent investment does not appear to be as beneficial as using the $100 to pay down your mortgage. Over the life of the loan, the total net cost after backing out the investment you would have is $393,170 compared to $379,604 per Chart No. 3. However, if you assume that you could earn 10 percent on your investment, your net cost drops to $315,085 and thus is a better investment than accelerating your loan payment.

Obviously, this is a decision that requires consultation with your tax preparer in order to determine which plan is better for you.

The preceding charts demonstrate how much a house will cost you after 20 or 30 years of payments and *not the price you would pay if you paid cash for it.* You can say, *"We bought* a house for $200,000 cash," or you can say, *"We are buying* a $200,000 house that will cost us $438,633 by the time we pay for it if we pay only the scheduled required payments."

It is pointed out several times in this book that many people feel when they can buy something on credit, it is a sign they can afford it. That is not so. That is not the test to use when deciding whether or not you can afford something. The test is what you can afford — not the method of payment. This test also applies when borrowing to buy a house. Don't let easy credit be your guide to what you can afford.

A bank or savings and loan might advise you that you are "qualified" for a certain loan. That might be true from the lender's viewpoint, but not from yours.

The lender will feel secure because the mortgage on your home can be foreclosed and the home taken away from you if you don't pay. That would be a tough way to discover you have purchased more home than you can afford. Study carefully to make sure when you go into debt for anything that you can make the payments *comfortably.*

Many experts in the real estate industry have indicated that most homebuyers tend to "stretch" themselves to the maximum when it comes to buying a house.

Consider the wisdom of purchasing a less expensive home with smaller mortgage payments and *investing* the difference over the life of the loan. You will thus be having a mortgage loan which is *decreasing and a separate valuable investment asset which is increasing.*

Rather than paying too much for too long for a house, you might get greater future pleasure by managing your money more wisely. Here's how you might do that. Calculate how much money you have available monthly over and above your living expenses.

Then use part of the money for a house payment and the balance for a monthly investment that will grow and be of benefit in future years.

The choice is yours! The following two charts demonstrate the difference between financing a $150,000 mortgage versus financing a $136,689 mortgage with the monthly payment difference of $100 being deposited in an investment earning 6 percent.

HOME WITH A $150,000 MORTGAGE WITHOUT AN INVESTMENT PLAN

Monthly required payment $1,127

Total payments over 30 year mortgage at 8.25% $405,684

Additional amount invested per month at 6% $0

Total investment value at end of 30 years $0

HOME WITH A $136,689 MORTGAGE AND AN INVESTMENT PLAN	
Monthly required payment	**$1,027**
Total payments over 30 year mortgage at 8.25%	**$369,684**
Additional $100 invested per month at 6% for 30 years	**$36,000**
Total investment value at end of 30 years	**$100,452**

As demonstrated by the examples, the same total amounts will be disbursed over the 30 years. However, under the second example, the individual will have $100,452 in an investment account at the end of the 30 years.

One of the biggest problems will be in estimating *what your income is going to be in the years ahead.* If you overestimate what your income is going to be, you will wind up with payments on your mortgage that are too high for you. On the other hand, if you underestimate what your income is going to be, you will wind up with a smaller house than you could afford.

A good solution is to estimate your future earnings on the low side and build or buy a house based on those estimated earnings. If your earnings become greater than you anticipated, you can always move up to a larger house. It is fun to move "up," but tough to have to move "down." Another alternative is to build or buy a house to which you can add an addition when you can afford it.

CLOTHING

In purchasing clothing, as with many other items, be careful about trying to "Keep up with the Joneses!"

The purchase of clothing is another subject that seems simple, but can be very complex. It has to be studied and analyzed from several angles. The objective is to determine the stores, the departments and the lines of clothing that fit *your* money management plan.

One of the best things you can do is to visit several stores when *you are not buying* to get a better understanding of the various lines and prices they offer. *Your ultimate objective is to be a very intelligent buyer.*

Visiting with relatives, neighbors, friends and fellow workers about where they shop will give you a better understanding of where you can get the best buys for *your* family.

You also will gain by being a student of the advertising and sales programs of various stores. Most stores sell a large percent of their clothing at the times of their maximum mark-up and profit margin. Good examples are the fall merchandise at the *beginning* of the fall season and spring merchandise at the *beginning* of spring.

Stores generally get their lowest profits at the *end of the various seasons*. For example, fall and winter prices are lowest at the *end* of that period. Be realistic that the selection of sizes and colors probably will not be as good. This is the time stores are selling items at a lower price because they do not want to carry them in inventory until the following year.

Some stores have so many sales it is difficult to know *when a sale price is really a sale price.* Watch the ads, and you will learn each store's pattern on sales and advertising. Some stores have sales when their sales of an item have not been up to expectations and they cut prices to sell excess inventory.

Some stores receive merchandise, mark it up to a high price and immediately put it on sale at a lower price. This is an example of a sale not being a genuine sale.

Stores generally have few sales employees to help you, but there are managers or assistant managers in each department. You will benefit greatly from getting acquainted with them. They probably know when the next sale will be and are generally cooperative in sharing the information.

Pick out the item you want and ask when the item might be on sale. You will take a chance someone will buy it at the regular price and it will not be available when the sale occurs. You may be disappointed sometimes, but will save money other times.

The groceries chapter advises you not to go grocery shopping when you are hungry. The same advice should be applied when buying clothing. Don't wait until you *have to have* something to wear today or tomorrow.

When shopping, you will find many products that are very similar and equal in quality but sold at different prices. The difference in price is due to the amount of advertising and promotion and the prestige of the designer's name.

There are some famous-name products in stores that have a strong following among all ages, particularly teenagers. A sweatshirt with a famous name may cost two or three times what a plain sweatshirt of the same quality might cost. Can you afford the cost of the prestige?

Purchasing clothing at retail stores is not the only way to obtain what you need. Many schools, churches and other groups have "swapping days" where you can trade clothes your children have outgrown for sizes they now need. Other good buys for used clothing can be found at rummage sales, garage sales, thrift shops and consignment shops. Choose the course of action that is best for you.

GROCERIES

The point is made many times in this book that expenses generally fit into two categories — ESSENTIAL and DISCRETIONARY. Groceries would at first seem to fit into the ESSENTIAL category because they give our bodies needed sustenance to maintain our bodies in good condition.

Grocery stores have many items of varying quality and prices, all of which will sustain us. When that fact is accepted, many items in grocery stores change from ESSENTIAL to DISCRETIONARY. The degree to which expenses are ESSENTIAL or DISCRETIONARY do change at various income levels.

The amount of money going through the grocery category makes it very important to *spend very wisely* every dollar and penny. Here are four big reminders!

Don't go to a grocery store —

1. Without a definite list of your needs.
2. Without a definite limit on the amount you plan to spend.
3. When you are hungry.
4. Every day or so. You will be better organized and save money if you go grocery shopping once a week.

The items sold in grocery stores pose lots of temptations to wreck your money management plan.

Discipline yourself to stick to your list and your dollar spending limit.

An increasing number of shoppers have spent a few dollars on small calculators and take them along as they go through the aisles. They add the price of each item as they put it in their baskets.

This prevents "checkout counter shock." *Know* what is really *essential* and what is just a *fun* or *impulse* purchase on your part. Don't apologize for having a money management system.

Coupons are now available for many grocery items. If there is a coupon available for an item you definitely *need* — *do* use the coupon. On the other hand, don't let a coupon entice you into buying something that you really don't need.

Don't apologize for using coupons. As you clip coupons, file them in an envelope, perhaps with alphabetical compartments. File generally by brand name and take your envelope with you to the store. Develop your own type of envelope.

In their pricing structure, the people who sell products know they should sell a product for a certain price to make a desired profit. They use coupons to encourage people to buy an item and include the cost of coupons in the shelf price.

If you use coupons, you are taking advantage of the savings available to you. If you don't use the coupons, you are making it possible for *other people* to take advantage of the lower net prices resulting from the use of coupons.

Stores sometimes offer "buy one, get the second free." This is another savings opportunity if it is a product you need and will use. But don't buy it just because of the price.

Many families say they save $10 or more per week — over $500 per year — by using coupons. Be good to your family!

Have a definite system for replenishing your inventory of the staple items you want to keep on hand, such as coffee, milk, butter, bread, cereal, etc. The better you plan your buying list, the less you will be tempted to buy items you really don't need.

Pay attention to the cost per ounce calculations on the price tags of various items. Sometimes it is wise to buy the size with the lowest price per ounce. At other times it might not be wise to buy the item with the lowest cost per ounce. Don't let the lower cost per ounce trick you into buying more of that item than you really need.

The French word for "caution" is "advertisse-ment," spelled slightly different from our American word "advertisement." Pay attention to advertising, but don't let it lead you into unwise purchases.

Industry sources have reported that among the items in grocery stores on which Americans spend the most are *beef, soft drinks, chicken and cereal.* Just manage wisely.

The type of grocery store will have an important effect on the amount you spend. If it is a "no-frills" store that advertises lower prices, and you are confident their prices are lower, you will save money by shopping there.

A more upscale store will generally charge a bit more for the same items because they feel they provide greater service and availability of items. The top-scale store will charge more on an average for their products. *Do your own survey on identical items you frequently buy and it will tell you where to shop.*

You also can save by one well-planned shopping trip per week at the store with the best prices instead of shopping three or four times per week at a more convenient store.

Americans are in love with fast food or already prepared foods. That is fine as long as people understand what the costs are to them and what the alternatives might be. A general average in the restaurant business is that the cost of the ingredients is approximately 30 to 35 percent of the price on the menu. That means a restaurant, fast food establishment or grocery store delicatessen is getting paid approximately 65 percent of their selling price for their overhead,

126

labor and profit in preparing the food. On that basis, the more food preparation you do at home, the more you will save.

Another way to keep expenses down is for the family to have a cooking session over the weekend where an assortment of dishes can be prepared for enjoyment during the coming week. This will be particularly beneficial if Mom has a job outside the home.

This might give Mom a break and the husband and children the opportunity to demonstrate their cooking skills. The family spends time together in the process. It also will be great training for the children!

"COOKING JAMBOREE"

An expansion of the above idea might be two families having a "Cooking Jamboree" once a month where each might cook twenty or more entrees that can be placed in a freezer and enjoyed throughout a month.

Some of the favorite entrees might be served two or three times in a month and others only once or twice in a month. A variety of easy to fix salads, side dishes and desserts could be added each day to produce a variety of delicious dinners.

Under this plan the head cook will save at least 20 to 30 hours of time per month along with very important savings in the purchase of groceries.

That is a combination of benefits that is hard to beat!

In checking with our public library we found three books that will be very helpful on this type of project.

Title:
The Best Freezer Cookbook
(Freezer-friendly recipes, tips and techniques)
Author: Jan Main
Publisher: Rose R., 2001

Title:
Month of Meals (One day to a freezer full of entrees)
Author: Kelly Machel
Publisher: KRM Publishing, 1997

Title:
Fresh From The Freezer (Make-ahead gourmet)
Author: Michael Roberts with Janet Spiegel
Publisher: Morrow, 1990

AUTOMOBILES

Automobiles rank high as wreckers of financial plans for many individuals and families. They also set the stage for great long-term savings.

There is a big caution about buying cars. It is to buy a car in the price range you can afford rather than getting into a contest to see whether you or your neighbors or fellow workers can drive the most expensive car.

Don't apologize to anyone for buying a car in the price range you can afford or for buying a used car where major depreciation (decline in value) has already occurred and there will be less depreciation in value in the years ahead. This is especially true for a second car or a car for a high school or college student.

Do be embarrassed if you let yourself get involved in pride or false pride and buy a car you really can't afford. Cars are classic examples of people trying to "Keep up with the Joneses." Sometimes they seem to present the challenge of "Going One Better Than The Joneses."

Automobile dealers have great assortments of cars in all price ranges. They like to please their customers by selling cars the customers like the most.

Keep in mind, however, that the dealers are not in charge of your money management system. It is up to *you* to determine what fits with *your* financial planning.

There are also other factors to be considered in connection with cars. Over and above the cost of a car are the annual dollars of depreciation, taxes involved based on the value of the car, gasoline or other fuel consumption, insurance and general upkeep. Insurance rates are necessarily high. Don't overload yourself or a teenager with these factors.

Many teenagers work and offer to pay part of the costs of a car. It is important young people know what the costs are going to be *before* they make their commitment. They need to develop a money management system to know how they are going to provide their share of the costs.

The total variations in cost can be hundreds or thousands of dollars per year between higher priced and lower priced cars. Know what a car *really* costs!

As indicated earlier, the decline in market value of a car from year to year is called depreciation. The estimated depreciation on each vehicle is based on information from several industry used car value guidebooks. Every dealer has these books. Cars *do* depreciate. Become more knowledgeable about depreciation!

Leasing a car sometimes looks attractive because the monthly lease payment is less than a payment on a loan to purchase a car. Keep in mind when you lease a car, you only have lease payment receipts at the end of the lease and the dealer still owns the car. If you buy a car with payments due, you get to keep the car after all payments are made. Study all the figures! Know what you are spending and what you are receiving. If necessary, have a credit counselor or financial planner help you make your calculations!

If you are buying a new car and are not experienced in buying cars, you might do yourself a profitable favor by utilizing the services of *Consumer Reports Price Service.* For a fee of $12 they will give you the dealer's *net cost*, after discounts and allowances to the dealer, not the frequently advertised "invoice price." Their address is CONSUMER REPORTS, P.O. Box 450927, Chicago, IL 60654. You can also get information from the Internet. After you get this information, get the assistance of a very tough negotiator if you don't have those qualifications.

A current trend in the automobile industry is to charge no interest on the financing. *That is fine if you are also getting all of the discounts previously available.* If you don't get those discounts you are paying no or less interest instead of getting the discounts. Get the lowest possible cash price on the car and then the lowest financing costs.

The important dollar figure is the *total dollar cost* whether it be cost after discounts plus cost of financing or cost without financing charges.

It is also important to remind you that if you get "no-interest financing" to be sure you make all payments *on or before* the due date of each payment.

Some of the paperwork on that type of financing provides that if you make any payment later than the due date you will have to pay interest on the total obligation. Read the paperwork very carefully and act accordingly.

VALUABLE INFORMATION
FROM THE AAA

At this point we are privileged to present valuable information from the AAA. The AAA is a federation of motor clubs serving 43 million members in the United States and Canada through more than 1,100 offices. It was originally called the American Automobile Association but now simply the AAA. That name is usually followed by the name of the state in which the local office is listed. In telephone directories the listings will probably be AAA Kansas, AAA Arizona, AAA Mid-Atlantic, etc.

AAA can best be described as "The Motorist's Friend." They provide a wide range of services including information on highway travel, hotels, resorts, motels, restaurants and sightseeing points of interest. One of their important services is emergency road assistance when troubles develop. They also have a full service travel agency and an insurance department.

AAA also conducts research projects on a wide range of subjects of interest to motorists. A recent study reported in the *AAA* brochure *YOUR DRIVING COSTS 2002* covered the costs of owning and operating three top selling cars in three price levels.

In their research, AAA used three cars as examples of prices on four door sedans, a Mercury Grand Marquis selling for approximately $25,000, a Ford Taurus in the $20,000 range and a Chevrolet Cavalier in the $15,000 range.

There are other makes of cars in these price ranges so we are using only dollar figures at the heads of the columns on the following form.

EXAMPLES OF THE TOTAL COSTS OF AUTOMOBILES

	$25,000 Car	$20,000 Car	$15,000 Car
OWNERSHIP COSTS	PER YEAR	PER YEAR	PER YEAR
Comprehensive insurance ($250 deductible)	$174	$144	$200
Collision insurance ($500 deductible)	$358	$321	$391
Bodily injury and property damage ($100,000, $300,000, $50,000)	$484	$484	$484
License, registration, taxes	$238	$203	$162
Depreciation (15,000 miles annually)	$4,420	$3,706	$3,037
TOTAL OWNERSHIP COSTS	$5,674	$4,858	$4,274

OPERATING COSTS	PER MILE	PER MILE	PER MILE
Gas and oil* *At $1.34 per gallon	6.5 cents	5.9 cents	5.2 cents
Maintenance	4.3 cents	4.1 cents	3.9 cents
Tires	2.2 cents	1.8 cents	1.5 cents
Cost Per Mile (15,000 Miles Annually)	13.0 cents	11.8 cents	10.6 cents
TOTAL OPERATING COSTS	$1,950	$1,770	$1,590

TOTAL OWNERSHIP AND OPERATING COSTS PER YEAR	$7,624	$6,628	$5,864

Figures on the cost of ownership and cost of operation are courtesy of AAA.

As indicated on the chart, there are two factors to consider in how much a car costs. The first is the *Cost of Ownership*. This starts with the total cost of the car whether it be for cash, payments due without interest or payments due with interest. It also includes the various types of insurance necessary, license, registration and taxes and very importantly, *depreciation*. All of these figures need to be developed on an annual basis so they can be compared to similar costs on other less expensive or more expensive cars.

The second factor to consider is the *Operating Costs* on an annual basis. This involves fuel, maintenance and tires on the cost per mile based on an average of 15,000 miles per year.

The total of these two factors, Cost of Ownership and Operating Costs, thus become your Total Annual Cost for each car to compare with other cars.

For example, the annual cost of a car in the $20,000 range will be $996 less than the car in the $25,000 range. Similarly there will be a savings of $764 by buying a car in the $15,000 range instead of the $20,000 range. The total savings on one car is great, but the savings on two cars is greater, and most families do have two cars.

By achieving these savings *you open another big door of opportunity*. Estimate your savings on an annual basis and divide by 12 to determine your monthly savings. Deposit or invest that amount monthly, compounded monthly at 5 percent per year, and you will accumulate sizable amounts through the years, as indicated on the following chart.

GROWTH OF MONEY FROM SAVINGS ON AUTOMOBILES

Annual savings between a $20,000 car and a $15,000 car	Monthly savings and deposit	Will grow to these amounts in the number of years indicated compounded monthly at 5 percent per year.			
		10	20	30	40
$764	$64	$9,980	$26,416	$53,487	$98,072

Annual savings between a $25,000 car and a $20,000 car	Monthly savings and deposit	Will grow to these amounts in the number of years indicated compounded monthly at 5 percent per year.			
		10	20	30	40
$996	$83	$12,942	$34,258	$69,366	$127,188

Total savings on two cars	Monthly savings and deposit	Will grow to these amounts in the number of years indicated compounded monthly at 5 percent per year.			
		10	20	30	40
$1,760	$147	$22,922	$60,674	$122,853	$225,260

After reviewing the figures on the cars in the $15,000, $20,000 and $25,000 price ranges it will be easy to realize the figures on savings by moving down from the $35,000 and up price ranges would be substantially higher.

We are not suggesting this policy of selecting cars be only on a one time purchase or for a few years. We suggest that it be a long range policy established at your earliest possible age so you can calculate the growth of your savings over a period of many years.

ENCOURAGEMENT FROM AAA

Marketing messages in our automotive culture often urge people to "drive bigger," "go faster" and "do more." Such messages can be inconsistent with fuel conservation, traffic safety, vehicle wear and tear and a healthy environment.

The car or truck you drive, how it's maintained, where you drive and how you drive are the most important factors in conserving fuel and staying safe behind the wheel.

HOUSEHOLD EXPENSES AND OTHER HINTS

Here are some money-saving ideas for your consideration.

— Turn off your lights, TVs and radios when they are not being used. You can buy something enjoyable for your family with the savings.

— Use your dishwasher or laundry washer and dryer *only* when you have a full load of dishes or clothing. The cycle costs about the same whether you have a light load or a full load.

— If you have an old-fashioned clothesline or an indoor rack, dry laundry that way when there is no rush.

— Pets are important to many people, but they can be *very expensive.* One dollar per day for dog food will cost $365 per year. That amount compounded monthly at 5 percent will increase to $4,723 in 10 years and $46,416 in 40 years. Also remember, veterinarians do charge for their services. *Just know your costs.*

— Plan your food preparations so you have no leftovers that can't be saved and served later.

— Carpooling can save you bundles of money. *Driving to and from work all by yourself is the most expensive luxury for many people!* If your work hours are consistent, try to ride with your fellow workers or have them ride with you. You can save $500 or more per year. Don't rule out savings by using public transportation. As pointed out earlier in the chapter *"How Money Grows,"* $50 per month in savings will grow to $8,194 in 10 years and $99,575 in 40 years. Is that important to you and your family?

— A home computer can help make your money management easier and be valuable computer training at the same time.

— Here's an idea on getting a special "bonus" by having a money management system. If you have a strict system, it will make it easy to say "no" to friends and relatives who want to borrow money. You can truthfully say to them, "We operate on a very strict system, and there is no place in our system for us to make loans."

— "Brown bagging" can save you money. If you work in an office, factory or warehouse where you can take your lunch, it will save you many dollars. Be proud of *your* money-saving ideas!

POP AND OTHER BEVERAGES

Beverages present another great opportunity to save money!

The amount of space grocery stores are dedicating to sales of soft drinks is a good indication of the amount of money people are spending on those beverages.

It seems that many men, women and children just have to have a can or bottle of pop in their hands throughout the day. They probably have not realized the total costs involved.

There may be nothing wrong from a health standpoint, but the effects on your money management system can be monumental.

If a person drinks just one can of pop per day at a vending machine price of 75 cents, the cost per year will be $273.75. That amount saved and compounded monthly will grow to $34,812 in 40 years. If four people in a family each do the same, the amount per year will be $1,095! That amount of money would grow in a savings or investment account to $139,249 in 40 years.

Doing without one, two, three or four cans of pop at a vending machine price of 75 cents and saving that amount for 30 days, depositing it in a savings account at 5 percent interest per year, compounded monthly, will grow to the amounts indicated on the following chart.

140

IF THE COST OF ONE, TWO, THREE OR FOUR CANS OF POP AT 75 CENTS PER CAN IS SAVED AND DEPOSITED MONTHLY IN A SAVINGS ACCOUNT AT 5% INTEREST PER YEAR, COMPOUNDED MONTHLY, THE AMOUNT WILL GROW AS INDICATED BELOW

Years	1 Can 75 Cents	2 Cans $1.50	3 Cans $2.25	4 Cans $3.00
10 years	$3,542	$7,085	$10,627	$14,169
20 years	$9,377	$18,753	$28,130	$37,507
30 years	$18,986	$37,972	$56,957	$75,943
40 years	$34,812	$69,624	$104,437	$139,249
50 years	$60,878	$121,758	$182,635	$243,513

Many people like to have a drink of liquor, beer or wine. If you enjoy a drink, select the brands carefully — know your cost — practice *moderation* — and you will save money. *Moderation* is the key!

CIGARETTES

CONGRATULATIONS if you don't smoke! You are on your way to a fortune. It can be done!

Cigarettes present a big savings opportunity for those who smoke and those who are in the process of deciding whether or not to smoke.

This is not about the possible detriment to one's health. This is about the adverse effects on your money management system.

Cigarettes are now selling for about $4.25 per pack or more, depending on the state tax. If, instead of buying that one pack per day, a person would save that amount of money for 30 days, deposit it in a savings account, compounded monthly at 5 percent per year, the savings would be $1,587 in a year.

Those figures are for just *one pack* per day. The following chart shows how this $4.25 per pack savings from not smoking one, two, or four packs per day would grow. This presumes the daily savings are deposited monthly in a savings account compounded monthly at 5 percent per year in 10, 20, 30, 40 and 50 years.

THE FOLLOWING CHART IS BASED ON THE COST OF CIGARETTES BEING AN AVERAGE OF $4.25 PER PACK, WITH THE DAILY SAVINGS BEING DEPOSITED MONTHLY IN A SAVINGS ACCOUNT, COMPOUNDED MONTHLY AT 5% PER YEAR			
YEARS	ONE PACK	TWO PACKS	FOUR PACKS
10	$20,074	$40,148	$80,296
20	$53,136	$106,272	$212,544
30	$107,586	$215,172	$430,344
40	$197,270	$394,540	$789,080
50	$344,978	$689,956	$1,379,912

Young men or women getting their first job at the current minimum wage will get a big reminder of the cost of smoking when they realize almost 16 percent of their earnings, after income taxes, would be needed for one pack per day. They would have to work a bit more than *one hour* out of an *8-hour day* to buy one pack.

THE PERCENT OF NET INCOME, AFTER TAXES, FOR AN INDIVIDUAL OR COUPLE THAT MIGHT BE SPENT FOR CIGARETTES OR AVAILABLE FOR OTHER PURCHASES OR INVESTMENT.

Hourly And Annual Income (40 Hrs. Per Wk.)	Approx Income Taxes*	Approx Net Income After Taxes	One Pack Per Day $1,587** Yearly	Two Packs Per Day $3,174** Yearly	Four Packs Per Day $6,348** Yearly
($5.15) $10,712	$755	$9,957	15.94%	31.88%	63.75%
($6.00) $12,480	$1,083	$11,397	13.92%	27.85%	55.70%
($7.00) $14,560	$1,467	$13,093	12.12%	24.24%	48.48%
($8.00) $16,640	$836	$15,804	10.04%	20.08%	40.17%
($9.00) $18,720	$1,221	$17,499	9.07%	18.14%	36.28%
($10.00) $20,800	$1,606	$19,194	8.27%	16.54%	33.07%
$25,000	$2,383	$22,617	7.02%	14.03%	28.07%
$30,000	$3,308	$26,692	5.95%	11.89%	23.78%
$40,000	$5,158	$34,842	4.55%	9.11%	18.22%
$50,000	$7,269	$42,731	3.71%	7.43%	14.86%
$75,000	$15,210	$59,790	2.65%	5.31%	10.62%
$100,000	$23,822	$76,178	2.08%	4.17%	8.33%

*Federal and State income tax estimates are based on persons being single in the lower bracket, and married (no dependents) with persons with income beginning at $16,640 and higher.

**The amount of savings or cost per year is based on the cost of 1, 2 or 4 packs per day at $4.25 per pack being saved, invested and compounded monthly at 5 percent per year.

On the preceding chart, married tax rates are used for annual incomes of $16,640 ($8 per hour) and above.

The amount of savings or cost per year in the chart is based on the cost of one, two or four packs at $4.25 per pack per day being saved and invested monthly, and compounded monthly at 5 percent per year.

Yes! You can save hundreds of thousands of dollars.

If the savings are compounded monthly at *8 percent*, the totals from not smoking become sensational as illustrated by the following chart.

Investment Growth for Fifty Years	One Pack	Two Packs	Four Packs
8% Return	$820,264	$1,640,528	$3,281,056

Review "Teaching Children Money Management" for a reminder how compounding of interest makes money "grow."

A SAD REFLECTION

Many people take the position they can't afford life, health and disability insurance but feel they can afford to smoke.

HOBBIES, ENTERTAINMENT AND A BIG ETC.

The chapter "Teaching Children Money Management" stressed the importance of parents teaching their children how to make choices on how they spend their money. Research has disclosed that many adults do not fully realize the opportunities *they* have to make choices.

As we begin this chapter it is timely to remind you of the choices you have in spending your money. It is difficult to describe the subjects of this chapter as essential when most of them are *highly discretionary.*

As part of your money management, it is strongly suggested that *every* person, couple and family become more mindful of the choices they do have.

Choices change with the ages of the people involved, their incomes, their employment and social situations. People are encouraged to see their dentist twice a year. You are encouraged to review many times a year the choices you have in spending your money. Don't let yourselves get in the T.H.W.A.D.I. thinking groove. That is pronounced THWAH-DEE. It means "That's How We've Always Done It."

In interviewing people about their money management, it became clear that everyone feels the things *they* enjoy should be classified as *essential* or NEEDS. At the same time, those same people question the judgment of their acquaintances who also consider the things *they* like as *essential*. Those appraisals can be classified as "just human nature" to favor ourselves with one standard but apply a different standard to others.

Ask a man who plays golf at every opportunity and he will present a case for it being *essential*. He will say he is protecting his health by taking exercise. He is saving money by exercising instead of paying doctor's bills. He is performing his office or other work with greater efficiency as a result of his recreational time. He is developing business contacts on the golf course that are very beneficial to him and his family. Almost everyone seems to do a good job of justifying the things *they* like as essential. Be *honest* with yourselves!

Telephone and television services provide a good study in *essential* vs. *discretionary* expenses.

A good question might be, "Are telephone and television services, over and above basic connections, essential or discretionary — NEEDS vs. WANTS?" The first response would be, "essential." The word "discretionary" would follow and then be followed by the words, "But we *like* those services."

It is appropriate to say that every home in the United States should have a telephone and a TV. It is equally appropriate to say the amount spent on telephone and television services should be limited to what families *should* spend in relation to their income and the services that are clearly *essential* — *NEEDED* — by the family.

When a telephone or television service provides convenience, pleasure and entertainment, it gets very difficult not to consider it essential. If, but only if, the amount of expense is *no problem* for a family, the decision is easy. When the telephone and television or other expenses prevent the family from having the money for clearly essential items, the family needs to take a new reading on what is most important for the family. Under that circumstance, limit the definition of *essential* to the most *basic of services.*

For telephone service, that would be *one* telephone that would allow for important messages and emergency communications. For television, it would be *one* TV with an antenna to receive local stations.

It would be difficult to discontinue something to which the family has become accustomed. Just considering *needs* versus *wants*, however, will strengthen your judgment on future decisions on a wide range of subjects.

The phone, television and other services available are very tempting, but they are not free. Consider whether *each* of the services is essential or discretionary.

The Caller I.D. service is interesting, but it does cost money. If you have a *very strong rea-*

148

son, other than fun, to "screen" calls before answering the phone, the Caller I.D. system might be a need for you. If it is just a fun thing to know who is calling, it becomes a discretionary expense. Too often it is used to not answer calls from people who are trying to collect debts. How well did you do before Caller I.D. became available?

The telephone company provides services such as Call Forwarding, Call Waiting, Three-way Calling, Call Return, Auto Redial and other services. Study them carefully. Analyze whether they are worth the money to you in *dollars and cents*. $15 per month or $180 per year will buy many things for which a family has an *essential* need. If the money is saved and deposited, it will *grow* to a significant amount in a few years.

Did you live and survive before these services became available? That may be a good way to test the degree to which they are essential or discretionary. If money is limited in a family it becomes a matter of choices — some easy and some tough.

Long distance rates have come down but still can account for many dollars if you don't keep your guard up. If you are more than a very slight user of long distance calls, you might consider the following ideas.

Plan your call. Think of the subjects you plan to talk about. If there is more than one or two subjects, put your list in writing. Cover each subject, but don't get involved in repetition. Unfortunately, many people do. One study indicated that 43 percent of phone calls involve *repetitious subjects*. Cover one subject and go on to the next.

We are well into the cellular phone age. They have become a subject requiring more attention by many users. Know and be guided by all of the details of the service you bought.

We now present the word "cell-a-holic" to describe a person who has a compulsion for "living" on a cell phone. Save some of that money for you to enjoy later for many important things.

Another budget buster for many families is entertainment in its many forms. There are many sports to play or watch. There are plays, musicals, video games, bingo, gambling, trips and hobbies that are enjoyable but expensive. The value of *each* type of entertainment has to be considered and choices made. Start by thinking you can't afford any of those things and let yourselves cautiously spend money on the most important uses.

Some people spend money on renting movies when the TV channels are loaded with movies and other programs. The movie rental business is big business. There is nothing wrong with renting movies if you can afford them.

One movie per week at $3 would cost $156 per year. Two a week would cost $312, and three a week would cost $468. The decisions are yours on what you can afford and how various items rate on your *priority* standards.

If you like to go to a movie theater, be realistic about what it costs. With most movie tickets at $6 or more, plus travel, snacks and incidentals, it's easy to spend $20 and up per couple for an evening. How high is that on *your* list of *needs*?

With the major television networks providing many fine programs from news to movies, sports events and assorted features, are you justified in paying for *additional television channels* available by cable?

Distinguish between what is *fun* for you and what is something you really *need*. What is the *value* in those additional channels? If having sufficient funds for other needs is a problem with you, how do more TV channels rate in your priorities when viewed in the light of essential versus discretionary items?

In the money management process there are important discretionary decisions that must be made by you. As with many subjects, it remains a matter of priorities! Would you prefer to have the services, the cash for something else or an investment that will grow? The decisions are yours.

151

Each family has to determine what is essential and what is discretionary for them. Don't be too easy on yourselves, particularly if you are having *any* difficulty in living within your income.

Money management is all about choices. That is *your* "department." Even if you are living within your income, there may be things that should get a higher priority, like more life insurance to protect your family or accumulating money you will need in your retirement years.

Be tough on yourselves in analyzing what is essential and what is discretionary. Consider the amounts you want to spend on the discretionary things you would *like to have or do* against the amounts of money for essential things you *need to have or do*. Then decide what is best for you.

LOTTERIES AND GAMBLING

Some of the words in the preface to this book were:

"It is not the purpose of this book to tell you how you should live your lives or spend your money. Its purpose is to present choices for your decisions."

That is a very difficult position to maintain when you are writing about gambling in general and the lottery in particular. The lottery now has become the fastest growing form of gambling.

What is gambling? One dictionary definition says that gambling is engaging in "reckless or hazardous behavior."

Among professional gamblers, the lottery has the reputation of being the most reckless form of gambling. The fact that it is generally for few dollars at a time might make it seem just a harmless form of recreation. If so, we should try to "sell" those players on a more profitable form of recreation.

The National Council on Problem Gambling reported that in just 20 years, revenues from legal wagering in the United States have grown by nearly 1,500 percent. In 1974 the National Council estimated that legal wagering amounted to $17 billion or about 1 percent of personal income in the United States. Gaming revenues were approximately $3 billion dollars.

By 1995 the amount wagered legally in the United States had reached $550 billion or 9 percent of United States personal income, and legal gaming revenues mounted to $44 billion.

The dollars of both the wealthy and low-income families can be lost, and families disrupted, when members become addicted to playing the lottery or other gambling.

Gambling locations take many forms, including casinos, the Internet, bars, service stations and grocery and convenience stores. More and more people are exposed to the thought of "winning big" despite the tremendous odds against them.

For the wealthy it may not be a financial problem, at least in the beginning. It can, however, lead to gambling addictions that can have serious family consequences, over and above losing a fortune.

Unfortunately, gambling and the lottery do the greatest damages to those with the greatest needs, the low-income families.

The government has recognized the damage to health from tobacco with a required warning on each package of cigarettes. Many people feel a warning of the odds against winning should be placed on all lottery tickets. They also would like to see warnings posted in casinos telling patrons what percent of the casino income is paid out. Enacting such laws for casinos may never be realized because many casinos are operated in name by Native Americans, and state laws do not apply to their casinos.

The big winners from gambling on many reservations are large corporations operating the casinos. Some of the corporations are highly profitable and are listed on the New York Stock Exchange. Their profits paint a clear picture that there are many more losers than winners in gambling.

Even for the most skillful gambler, the odds are always against winning. For lotteries, the odds on winning are much lower than on other forms of gambling.

It is understandable that people would like to "make a killing" and come up with a big winning when playing the lottery. But the odds are small, almost nonexistent.

One researcher and writer on gambling has said the odds of winning $1 million dollars on roulette are about one in two million. Also, you are seven times more likely to win $1 million playing roulette than you are to win $1 million on playing the lottery.

Bill Eadington, director of the Institution for the Study of Gambling and Commercial Gaming, has described the odds of winning a lottery. He says if you buy 100 tickets a week for your entire adult life, from 18 to 75, you would spend $291,200 and still have only a 1 percent chance of winning the lottery.

It is one thing if you have so much money that gambling will not deprive *your* family of its essential needs. It is another thing to gamble and, directly or indirectly, deprive your family of even one small item.

What amounts of money can be saved by placing the money in a savings account instead of being spent on the lottery? The following chart shows what can happen if money is not spent on the lottery but is invested in a savings account, paying 5 percent per year compounded weekly. The chart shows how amounts from $5 to $100 per week will grow if these amounts are invested weekly for periods ranging from 1 to 20 years.

THIS CHART SHOWS HOW AN AMOUNT PLACED IN A SAVINGS ACCOUNT AND COMPOUNDED WEEKLY AT 5% PER YEAR WILL GROW IN THE YEARS INDICATED					
Years To Grow	$5 Each Week	$10 Each Week	$25 Each Week	$50 Each Week	$100 Each Week
1 year	$264	$535	$1,337	$2,674	$5,348
5 years	$1,481	$2,962	$7,406	$14,812	$29,625
10 years	$3,383	$6,766	$16,914	$33,829	$67,658
15 years	$5,824	$11,649	$29,122	$58,244	$116,488
20 years	$8,959	$17,918	$44,795	$89,590	$179,179

The well-known radio commentator Paul Harvey featured a story about a minister who said a prayer before a legislative session of senators. His prayer reminded them of their mistakes. The prayer included this sentence: "You have exploited the poor and called it the lottery."

Is there a better description of the lottery than that statement?

Because they have less money, people on low incomes are more likely to face bankruptcy when they lose money through playing the lottery. Bankruptcy experts estimate that thousands of people a year are filing for bankruptcy protection because of gambling. In many instances it started with the purchase of one lottery ticket.

It is important to provide children a positive attitude toward family finances. Parents who purchase lottery tickets in the presence of their children and talk about winning "big" in the lottery convey a false message about sound money management.

Many people who buy a lottery ticket act as if they have already won. They like to dream aloud of what they will do when they win. On the surface this appears harmless. But is it really harmless to waste hours, days, weeks, months and years daydreaming that you might someday win and spending money that is needed for other things.

The dream of winning the lottery is eroding the American Dream of working hard, saving money and being successful.

Pathological gambling has been defined as "a progressive disorder characterized by a continuous or periodic loss of control over gambling; a preoccupation with gambling and with obtaining money with which to gamble; irrational thinking; and a continuation of the behavior despite adverse consequences."

The term "problem gambler" is used to describe those individuals who have difficulties because of gambling but who do not meet the criteria for pathological gambling. Problem gambling may represent an early stage of pathological gambling.

The National Council on Problem Gambling has stated that "existing studies have found high costs to the individual (indebtedness, deteriorating relationships with family and friends, depression and suicide attempts); to the family (emotional turmoil, stress-related illness, lack of financial support, neglect and divorce); and to society (lost work productivity, unpaid taxes, bankruptcies, white collar crimes such as theft and embezzlement and associated costs to the criminal justice system)."

If you know of anyone who might have a gambling addiction, have them contact:

National Council on Problem Gambling
P.O. Box 9419
Washington, D.C. 20016
Phone: 800-522-4700
Web site: www.ncpgambling.org

CREDIT CARDS

There are *three ways to describe* a credit card. A credit card is a piece of plastic that:

1. Gives you the convenience to pay at the end of the month for purchases made during the month that you could or *could not* afford.

2. Permits you to buy something during the month at a time when you don't have the money to pay for it. That is, in effect, a *temporary loan.* If you still don't have the money at the end of the month, the purchase becomes a *credit card debt* on which you pay a *very high interest rate.*

3. Permits you to borrow money at about twice or more the interest rate banks normally charge.

You and *only you* determine what kind of a credit card or cards you have *and how you use them.*

The first use of a credit card might provide convenience and assist in good financial record-keeping. The other two uses can contribute varying amounts of financial grief for users.

Credit cards cause more difficulties and hardships in the money management process than any other factor. A survey by the National Foundation For Credit Counseling based in Silver Spring, Md., reported that 33 percent of

Americans overspend and go into debt during the Christmas holiday period.

Approximately 80 percent of those people go into debt for at least $500. That is a real money management system wrecker.

These figures serve as a reminder of the importance of anticipating these needs and setting the money aside in *advance* of your purchases.

In 1990 the average household credit card balance was $2,985. By 2000 the average balance had more than doubled to $8,123.

Savings by our total population plummeted from 10.9 percent of disposable income in 1982 to -0.1 percent in 2000.

Despite the strong economy in the 1990s, bankruptcies reached record highs — greater than during the Great Depression of the 1930s. Much of the blame rests with credit card debt.

The point has been made in other chapters that many people mistakenly think that if they can charge something or buy something on credit, they can afford it. That is not so! The real test is whether people can *afford* something, not the *method of payment.*

Most credit cards charge 18 percent to 22 percent interest on unpaid balances. To know exactly what your interest rate is, check the APR (annual percentage rate) on your credit card statement.

When you get your credit card statement each month, the only *wise* thing you can do is to pay the *total* amount of the indebtedness by the due date — *not* just the minimum payment due.

The minimum monthly payment required is usually about 2 percent of the total amount due, with a minimum payment of $10. If you do not pay the total amount due, the interest on the remaining total due is frequently close to the minimum payment due.

The credit card issuers also assess a penalty of $25 to $35 for payments received after the monthly due date. At least some of them also increase the interest rate under those circumstances.

Paying just the *monthly minimum* means paying little more than the interest. That procedure may require *many years* to pay off a purchase charged to a credit card.

Paying off a credit card debt by making only the required minimum monthly payments is like walking many miles on a treadmill and expending much energy but just barely moving a few inches forward each month. If you do not pay the full amount by the due date each month, you are borrowing money at very high interest rates from the credit card company.

If you want to borrow money, make a smart choice. Go to a bank and borrow directly what you need at a much lower interest rate. When you borrow money directly from a bank, the interest rate will probably be about half what you will pay on a credit card debt.

If a bank declines to loan you the amount of your credit card debt, that would be a sign you should not borrow through a credit card. Few people seem to recognize the financial condition they get themselves into when they pay only the required minimum payment each month.

Many department stores have charge accounts that operate like credit cards. They require only a minimum payment per month and then generally charge you a high interest rate on the balance. Treat that type of charge account the same as a credit card and pay the *total* balance due every month. Some observers feel that a substantial percent of the profits of those stores comes from the high interest they charge on their charge accounts.

Let's start with two examples of how a credit card purchase works on a purchase of an item that would sell at a cash price of $100.

As explained previously, the costs of the item would still be $100 if the statement from the credit card company is paid in full and on time at the end of the month. If that is not done the picture then changes.

The credit card companies generally require a monthly payment of 2 percent of the balance with a minimum of $10. The $10 minimum would apply to the $100 purchase each month until the total amount is paid. In the meantime, there would be, for example, 18 percent interest on the unpaid balance.

Credit Card Chart No. 1 shows the $100 purchase being made in the first month, the $10 minimum being paid each month for 11 months, the amount of interest charged each month and the declining balance. The net result is that the item which could have been purchased for cash for $100 will cost $109.16 when purchased with a credit card with extended payments.

CREDIT CARD CHART NO. 1
RESULTS OF $100 CREDIT CARD DEBT WITH ONLY MINIMUM PAYMENTS PER MONTH IN ONE YEAR

Starting Balance $100	Monthly Payment	Interest	Principal Reduced	Remaining Balance
Month 1				$100.00
2	$10.00	$1.50	$8.50	$91.50
3	$10.00	$1.37	$8.63	$87.87
4	$10.00	$1.24	$8.76	$74.11
5	$10.00	$1.11	$8.89	$65.22
6	$10.00	$.98	$9.02	$56.20
7	$10.00	$.84	$9.16	$47.04
8	$10.00	$.71	$9.29	$37.75
9	$10.00	$.57	$9.43	$28.32
10	$10.00	$.42	$9.58	$18.74
11	$10.00	$.28	$9.72	$9.02
12	$9.16	$.14	$9.02	$0.00
TOTALS	$109.16	$9.16	$100.00	

163

If more people realized the credit card purchase price compared to a cash purchase, there would be fewer credit card purchases.

The total cost is less severe on a credit card purchase for a smaller amount because of the $10 minimum monthly payment required. The $10 monthly minimum requires faster payments on the total balance with less interest being paid because of the faster declining balance than only the 2 percent on larger balances. The $10 minimum thus is not directed toward one small purchase.

One way or another, there is a marked difference between a cash purchase and a credit card purchase. The same situation would repeat on a department store purchase on which interest is charged.

We next present Credit Card Chart No. 2, which presents a different picture of what happens when there are multiple purchases with the credit card and the 2 percent minimum is greater than the $10 minimum. This chart shows how the final cost of the item will increase if only the 2 percent is paid monthly.

Chart No. 2 is based on a purchase of a $100 item that is only a *portion* of a much larger total of items purchased. Based on this assumption, we have projected that the minimum payment amount does not apply and the cardholder pays a minimum of 2 percent. For ease of understanding, we have used 2 percent of the original balance instead of 2 percent of a declining balance.

164

CREDIT CARD CHART NO. 2			
Date	Payment Amount	Interest	Balance
			$100.00
1st Year	$24.00	$17.47	$93.47
2nd Year	$24.00	$16.22	$85.69
3rd Year	$24.00	$14.67	$76.36
4th Year	$24.00	$12.86	$65.22
5th Year	$24.00	$10.68	$51.90
6th Year	$24.00	$8.04	$35.94
7th Year	$24.00	$4.95	$16.89
8th Year	$18.19	$1.30	$0.00
TOTALS	$186.19	$86.19	

As demonstrated above, it takes almost 8 years to pay off the $100 debt. Based on these assumptions, this item would ultimately cost the individual $186.19.

Chart No. 3 gives you a more complete picture. Carefully study the chart. Don't rush! Make sure you completely understand it.

In Chart No. 3, the example starts with a purchase and debt of $1,200. The chart shows what happens to the credit card debt in one year when only the required minimum payment of 2 percent of the total is paid each month and interest of $1\frac{1}{2}$ percent per month (18 percent per year) is added to the total balance.

CREDIT CARD CHART NO. 3 RESULTS OF $1,200 CREDIT CARD DEBT WITH ONLY MINIMUM PAYMENTS PER MONTH IN ONE YEAR				
Starting Balance 1,200.00	Monthly Payment	Interest	Principal Reduced	Remaining Balance
Month 1	$26.40	$18.00	$8.40	$1,191.60
2	$26.22	$17.88	$8.34	$1,183.26
3	$26.03	$17.75	$8.28	$1,174.98
4	$25.85	$17.63	$8.22	$1,166.76
5	$25.67	$17.50	$8.17	$1,158.59
6	$25.49	$17.38	$8.11	$1,150.48
7	$25.31	$17.26	$8.05	$1,142.43
8	$25.13	$17.13	$8.00	$1,134.43
9	$24.96	$17.02	$7.94	$1,126.49
10	$24.78	$16.89	$7.89	$1,118.60
11	$24.61	$16.78	$7.83	$1,110.77
12	$24.44	$16.66	$7.78	$1,102.99
TOTALS	$304.89	$207.88	$97.01	

Chart No. 4 also starts with a total debt of $1,200. The chart shows what happens in the account in the first year, month-by-month, and then at 5, 10, 15 and 18 years.

CREDIT CARD CHART NO. 4 RESULTS OF $1,200 CREDIT CARD DEBT WITH ONLY MINIMUM PAYMENTS MADE PER MONTH OVER A PERIOD OF EIGHTEEN YEARS			
	TOTAL MONTHLY PAYMENTS	TOTAL INTEREST PAID	TOTAL PRINCIPAL REDUCED	PRINCIPAL BALANCE REMAINING
1 YEAR	$304.89	$207.88	$97.01	$1,102.99
5 YEARS	$1,297.08	$884.37	$412.71	$787.29
10 YEARS	$2,148.07	$1,464.59	$683.48	$516.52
15 YEARS	$2,760.90	$1,832.29	$928.61	$271.39
18 YEARS	$3,111.99	$1,911.99	$1,200.00	$0.00

Yes, after 18 years, the credit card holder has finally paid off the $1,200 original balance after paying $3,111.99.

Chart No. 5 shows what happens to a credit card debt of $3,000 in one year when only the required minimum payment of approximately 2 percent of the total is paid each month and interest of $1^1/_2$ percent per month (18 percent per year) is added to the total balance.

		CREDIT CARD CHART NO. 5 RESULTS OF $3,000 CREDIT CARD DEBT WITH ONLY MINIMUM PAYMENTS PER MONTH IN ONE YEAR		
Starting Balance 3,000.00	Monthly Payment	Interest	Principal Reduced	Remaining Balance
Month 1	$66.00	$45.00	$21.00	$2,979.00
2	$65.54	$44.69	$20.85	$2,958.15
3	$65.08	$44.37	$20.71	$2,937.44
4	$64.62	$44.06	$20.56	$2,916.88
5	$64.17	$43.75	$20.42	$2,896.46
6	$63.72	$43.44	$20.28	$2,876.18
7	$63.28	$43.15	$20.13	$2,856.05
8	$62.83	$42.84	$19.99	$2,836.06
9	$62.39	$42.54	$19.85	$2,816.21
10	$61.96	$42.25	$19.71	$2,796.50
11	$61.52	$41.94	$19.58	$2,776.92
12	$61.09	$41.65	$19.44	$2,757.48
TOTALS	$762.20	$519.68	$242.52	

Chart No. 6 shows the $3,000 credit card debt over a period of 1, 5, 10, 15 and 20 years.

CREDIT CARD CHART NO. 6 RESULTS OF $3,000 CREDIT CARD DEBT WITH ONLY MINIMUM PAYMENTS MADE PER MONTH OVER A PERIOD OF TWENTY YEARS			
	TOTAL MONTHLY PAYMENTS	TOTAL INTEREST PAID	TOTAL PRINCIPAL REDUCED	PRINCIPAL BALANCE REMAINING
1 YEAR	$762.20	$519.68	$242.52	$2,757.48
5 YEARS	$3,242.70	$2,210.93	$1,031.77	$1,968.23
10 YEARS	$5,370.16	$3,661.47	$1,708.69	$1,291.31
15 YEARS	$6,765.94	$4,613.14	$2,152.80	$847.20
20 YEARS	$7,681.68	$5,237.51	$2,444.17	$555.83

Yes — still owing $555.83 after paying $7,681.68 in 20 years on a beginning credit card debt of $3,000.

After credit card users study these charts, there is little need to repeat the caution to pay the total due each month rather than just the minimum required payments. If you can't pay the total due, then ask yourself if you really could have afforded the purchases of the goods, services or fun that started the credit card debt. Then don't make the same mistake again!

If you are in debt on your credit cards, you might very well be saying at this time, "Oh my! How are we going to get out of this situation?" Here are some possibilities.

Determine where you can cut your living expenses and calculate the *highest possible amount you can pay each month* to reduce the debt. The number of months and/or years to pay off the debt can then be calculated.

When the credit card statement arrives, write the check for the amount you have calculated you can pay each month.

Put your credit cards away until the debts are paid. Tape a note on the cards with the amounts you owe. This will remind you of your problem when you are tempted to use the cards again. If necessary, just destroy the cards.

You may have to reduce your *discretionary* spending, and even some of your expenses which you had considered *essential*, to produce your highest possible monthly payments.

If at all possible, get a bank or other loan to pay off the entire credit card balance. Your goal is to get a loan that can be repaid over a period of time with a much lower interest rate than you are paying on your credit card debt.

A home equity loan is a possibility, but that is a long-term payout with your home as collateral. You will lose your home if you fail to make those payments. Refinancing your car is another option.

As part of getting a bank loan, try getting the credit card company to accept a one-time settlement in full for less than the total amount due. Credit card issuers are reported to generally accept 70 percent to 85 percent of the balance due in full settlement for a past due account if the cardholder indicates bankruptcy is the only other solution. Caution! Do not make *any* false statements.

If you are unable to negotiate this type of settlement yourselves, your best course of action is to work through professional credit counselors. This is discussed more fully later in this book.

Any such settlement is likely to show on your credit record. That may later adversely affect your ability to do business with banks or stores where you might wish to establish credit. But you can, in time, reestablish your credit rating.

If all else fails, the only way you are going to get rid of the credit card debt is to pay more each month than you are required to pay. That will be a very slow process, but it may be the only solution.

Many credit card holders owe $3,000 or more. The following Chart No. 7 shows if you pay *$50 per month* more than the required amount, it will take you four years and two months to pay off the $3,000 debt.

CREDIT CARD CHART NO. 7 PAYING $50 EXTRA PER MONTH Time required to payoff credit card debts of varying amounts with a $50 monthly payment above required minimum monthly payment.					
Credit Card Debt	$1,000	$2,000	$3,000	$4,000	$5,000
Payoff Time	1 year 7 months	3 years 0 months	4 years 4 months	5 years 7 months	6 years 9 months

The chart also shows how long it will take to pay off credit card debts of $1,000, $2,000, $4,000 and $5,000.

Chart No. 8 shows that if you pay *$100 more* per month than the required amount, it will take you two years and three months to pay off the $3,000 debt. The payout period is shorter because you are avoiding the payment of much interest. That is the key.

The chart also shows how long it will take to pay off debts of $1,000, $2,000, $4,000 and $5,000.

CREDIT CARD CHART NO. 8 PAYING $100 EXTRA PER MONTH Time required to payoff credit card debts of varying amounts with a $100 monthly payment above required minimum monthly payment.					
Credit Card Debt	$1,000	$2,000	$3,000	$4,000	$5,000
Payoff Time	10 months	1 year 7 months	2 years 4 months	3 years 0 months	3 years 9 months

Later in this book is the chapter "A Method of Reducing Debts and Avoiding Bankruptcy." That chapter also includes working your way out of credit card debt.

The credit card companies and banks are constantly waging a campaign to get more customers. Book publishing companies discovered centuries ago their best prospects for book sales were people who had previously bought books. So, a person with one or two credit cards is likely to get more cards.

The issuers of credit cards are now using that idea and are constantly trying to get people to switch to their card. Some studies estimate that credit card holders and others may receive 30 credit card offers annually.

A common approach of credit card companies is to give a lower interest rate for a few months and use the lower rate as "bait" to get people to accept the new card.

Card users can get some temporary relief with lower interest rates on their credit card debts by accepting the new card. They will not, however, make any meaningful progress in getting their financial affairs in order unless they also pay much more than the "minimum due" during the period they have the low interest rate.

The chapter "Rent to Own" stresses the point, "There is no such thing as a free lunch." Sooner or later people get what they pay for and *only* what they pay for, directly or indirectly.

The giving of temporary lower interest rates on credit card debts might be likened to the former practice of tobacco companies giving free cigarettes to teenagers. The tobacco companies planned on making a profit in time by doing so.

One of the major problems with credit card debt is that consumers are starting at younger ages to rely on credit. The credit card companies are taking dead aim at college and university students. They are not just asking the students if they would like to have a credit card. They are baiting them with T-shirts and other inducements to accept a card.

Recent studies suggest that a college undergraduate's credit card debt averages $2,200, and graduate students carry an average of $5,800.

When credit card debt is combined with student loans, many students leave college starting with more debt than previous generations. With a reliance on credit cards already developed, the financial future for many young adults will become extremely difficult unless they make some realistic decisions about the use of credit.

Caution your children who are or soon will be going to college or entering the business world to avoid starting the credit card habit.

Many people seem to have a *compulsion* to get into credit card debt. How can people with this problem be described? Alcoholics have a compulsion to drink. An alcoholic is defined as one who has a "compulsive use of alcoholic drinks." That definition parallels the troubles of some credit card debtors, so a new descriptive word, *"debt-a-holic,"* is presented. A debt-a-holic could be defined as "one who is involved in continued excessive or compulsive use of credit card debts."

Just as there are ways to help an alcoholic, there are also treatments for debt-a-holics. The suggestions in this book can help reduce the need for debt by helping people understand what credit card debt can do to them and their families. Determine how much money you have for spending and don't incur debt you can't afford.

Consumer Credit Counseling Service is an agency that will assist individuals with major credit card debts. They have offices in many cities, and the location of their nearest office can be secured by calling 1-800-388-2227 or on the Internet at http://www.nfcc.org. An important first step is to admit, "We need help!"

OTHER "EASY CREDIT"

"Easy credit" causes difficulty for many people on practically everything sold.

Easy credit is not just a problem in credit card use or purchasing cars. It is a trap into which people can fall in many ways. Here are more examples that can lead to difficulties in maintaining a money management system.

"NO PAYMENT..."

Stores usually price merchandise at a price that will give them a reasonable profit if sold for cash or 30-day credit.

A store may advertise a product with no payment due for six months or one year. That might mean the store selling the product has raised the price over and above a normal selling price to get you to take advantage of the credit offering. You are paying interest on the purchase without it being called interest.

Don't be fooled. If the item is priced at $500 with no payment on the balance for six months, it is probable the fair market price of the product is actually about $475. To that is added an interest charge of about $25 for six months at an annual rate of 10 percent, but it is not called interest.

Another possibility is that the store has an excess of an item remaining in their inventory that did not sell as expected. The store could cut the selling price or give extended credit at the store's expense to move it out of their inventory. One way or another, they are offering you an enticement to buy something that may not be a wise purchase.

So many people like to purchase things on time payment plans that it is difficult to purchase them on a cash basis and get a discount for doing so. There are only a few stores, generally individually owned, that will reward you for paying cash at the time of purchase.

Be a prudent and wise purchaser! If you do purchase something on a time payment plan, at least know what the financing is costing you.

There are many retail stores, banks and other businesses that offer a wide variety of goods and services to consumers. As individuals and family members, you are those *consumers.*

There is nothing illegal about stores and institutions offering credit to consumers like you. On the other hand, you have to keep your guard up and purchase those goods or services in a wise way. *If credit is involved, you are directly or indirectly paying for that credit.* As is pointed out in the next article, "There is no such thing as a free lunch."

There are many goods and services available that are beneficial for some consumers. There are other goods and services available that are "traps" for inexperienced and unwise consumers.

"RENT TO OWN"

"Rent to own" is another example of easy but expensive credit.

This type of credit involves renting an item with little or no down payment and then making payments, for probably a very long time, before you own it.

If a product seems easy to buy on this basis, you can be sure you are going to pay high interest, in effect, for the privilege of buying in this manner.

About the beginning of this century there were taverns that offered a "free lunch." They advertised that people could eat lunch at no cost if they purchased beer or other beverages.

An analysis showed there was enough profit on the beverages to also provide the "free" food. This was the origin of the expression, *"There is no such thing as a free lunch."*

Easy credit is like that. Directly or indirectly, you are going to pay for what you get. If you buy a product with easy credit, you are going to pay for both the product *and* the easy credit.

The appealing thing about products available through "rent to own" establishments is that televisions, radios, appliances, furniture and other products are available with little or no down payment required.

What is required is a contract under which you agree to pay a certain amount each month toward the purchase of the product. These contracts should be read very, very carefully *before* you sign. Know the fair price for the item compared to the price *you are agreeing to pay.*

The "rent to own" establishments deserve a profit on the products they sell and for, in effect, loaning you the money to make the purchase.

They also deserve to be reimbursed for the risk they are taking in placing the product in your hands with little or no down payment.

It is legal, but you should understand all that is involved in such arrangements.

HOME EQUITY LOANS

The difference between the market value of your home and the remaining balance due on your mortgage is your "equity." It might sound like an appealing idea, that *if your home is worth more than the existing mortgage debt*, you can use that equity as security for borrowing money.

Through the years homeowners have been able to borrow an additional amount of money by placing a *second mortgage* on their home. Doing so has not been a complimentary thing to hear about friends or neighbors. The name "home equity loan" has removed some of that stigma. The fact remains that a second mortgage is still a second mortgage and should be avoided unless there is a clear-cut benefit from going into that additional indebtedness.

Many people are getting home equity loans to pay off credit card balances with their higher interest rates. That sounds like a good idea, but it loses its merits when people go right back into credit card debt at the high interest rates. It also appears that the borrowers on home equity loans too frequently believe that those loans offer an automatic tax break on the interest expense. As with all other indebtedness, go into debt only when there is a sound reason to do so.

If the additional money you are thinking of borrowing is going to be for a clearly *necessary purpose or an investment*, a home equity loan *might* be a good idea.

If it just means going deeper into debt, with additional monthly payments to be made, it is probably a bad idea. Don't be too easy on yourselves in your analysis of what is *essential* or *discretionary.* Go into debt with great caution.

All home equity loans are not unwise. If you are planning to use the money to make an investment that will produce more *profit* than the interest expense on the loan, there *might* be greater justification for the loan, but there should still be careful consideration.

A possibly better approach is to think of securing a home equity *"line of credit."* A line of credit is an agreement by a bank to loan you a specified amount if you wish to borrow it. With a loan, you will pay interest on the entire amount even though you do not use all of the money. With a line of credit, you only pay interest on the money you need and borrow. That comes after you thoroughly consider if the additional mortgage on your home and the proceeds will benefit you.

If you are going to use the money to purchase goods or services which are really not necessary and for which you otherwise would not have the money, it is probably unwise for you to get a home equity loan or use a line of credit for that purpose.

If you can't afford something without the home equity loan, it is probably a good sign you can't afford it with a home equity loan.

Home equity loans are another example of easy credit, which too frequently makes life more difficult. Home equity loans have become attractive because the interest paid *may* be a deduction on your income tax. Be sure to calculate the tax savings against the interest paid before you decide. Does that small tax benefit outweigh other considerations? And where will you get the money to make the payments on your new mortgage loan?

Think of a bank as being a business that "sells" you the use of money at a price. It may be unwise for you to "purchase" what the bank has to offer. Going into debt easily is a money trap into which many people fall. A debt is a debt no matter what sweet words are used to advertise it.

A special caution is expressed in getting a home equity loan from a bank or other financial institution that advertises loans of 125 percent or any high percent of your equity. Very simply, you are going deeper into debt and if you are unable to make your payments you will lose your home. Always bear in mind it is easier to go into debt than to work your way out.

"PAYDAY" LOANS

A new challenge to those who are having financial difficulties has emerged. It is called a "payday" loan.

It sounds good that people can get a loan to carry them until payday. The cost, however, of getting that loan is shocking when analyzed.

Based on the laws of the various states, a worker in need of cash to get to the next payday can, for example, borrow $100. The loan, due in 15 days, generally requires a repayment of $115.

The extra $15 gets into proper perspective when you calculate that a $15 charge for borrowing $100 for two weeks amounts to 365 percent interest on an annual basis. Yes, 365 percent! Try very hard to manage your money so you do not have to pay this.

The high interest rate is now legal in some states but puts a lot of pressure, with very expensive interest rates, on those who need this short-term help.

Even though this is legal, those who think they need temporary loans are encouraged to try to manage their earnings wisely. Thus they will not have to pay such a very high rate of interest to get by until the next payday.

SECOND CHANCE

Another system of borrowing money has developed which appeals to a special group of borrowers. It is called "second chance."

The borrowers in the group have taken bankruptcy or otherwise developed a poor credit record. The good part is that the lenders will give a person a "second chance" and loan them money. The bad part is that this type of loan involves greater risk for the lender so justifies a higher interest rate. It is legal but expensive.

The borrower gets a "second chance" but pays a high price for it. If people develop a poor credit record through bankruptcy or otherwise, the best thing they can do is to manage their money affairs very carefully and rebuild their credit record gradually so they do not have to pay a high interest rate on money they borrow.

CHILD CARE

While child care is only one of the expenses listed under the household account, it ranks very high among the most difficult subjects in money management for many families. Thoughtful advance planning and choices can help families deal effectively with this important issue.

With a large percentage of mothers employed outside the home, many families have child care expenses. As with all goods and services, child care quality and costs vary. Spend time exploring your options, and find care that will meet the unique needs of your family.

Perhaps the first consideration should be whether the cost of child care and other work-related expenses actually make it feasible for a mother with young children to work outside the home.

Some families have a choice, and, using careful money management, can save money if the mother stays home and cares for the children herself. Other families may not have this option for a variety of reasons. For these families, spending time discussing the matter and examining some possible alternatives may be helpful.

Some families are fortunate to have relatives that are willing and able to provide care for a young child while parents work. This arrangement can save the family the high cost of child care. However, sometimes care by relatives is not an option or the best choice for the child or family.

Sometimes parents are able to find employment that allows them to work flexible hours, such as 9 a.m. to 3 p.m., while children are in school. Other times parents work different days or shifts to cut down on the hours that child care will be needed. Although this solution may cut or help eliminate child care expense, it sometimes causes other issues in the family. All options should be carefully considered before a decision is made.

Most states regulate child care providers in some way. Parents that choose unregulated care can lose their federal tax deduction designed to help offset the cost of child care. Check to find out what your state requires of someone providing child care.

Because the quality of child care is so important and has a lasting effect on the well-being of your child, cost is not the only consideration. Cost is just one of several important things to consider.

Start exploring the options as soon as you know care will be needed. Give yourselves lots of time to plan and shop around for the best fit for your family.

You also may find your family qualifies for some help in paying the expense of child care.

This is if you meet certain income guidelines, even if both parents are employed, and you receive no other assistance. Some providers also help by offering a sliding fee scale or will enroll your child with a part-time schedule.

If you need additional information on child care options, contact your local resource and referral agency. They can offer you free information on selecting care and the options available in your community.

More and more parents are developing and utilizing skills that enable one or both parents to work at home rather than working outside the home. These home-based business options may include doing computer or other office work, selling by phone or making telephone surveys, graphic design, bookkeeping or accounting services.

If you are changing careers because of a new baby in the family, be certain that you are realistic about the earning potential of your home-based business. You may discover that you will save child care expenses, but your income may be decreased more than your personal child care savings.

You also need to be realistic about how many hours each day you will be able to work while still caring for your child. Benefits offered by employers (like health insurance) are also an important consideration when making this decision. Carefully explore your options and make an educated choice.

Having quality, dependable child care is extremely important to your family's well-being. If you work outside your home, having a child care arrangement that meets your needs may be costly but the best decision. Be creative in finding a solution.

For women or men who enjoy working with children, perhaps a career in child care is just the solution for which you are looking. This could be one that allows you to earn needed income for your family and spend time with your children while offsetting the high cost of child care. Your local resource and referral agency can answer your questions about a career in child care.

Carefully weigh your options and find the best possible fit for your family and your money management system.

SOME SPECIAL SAVINGS OPPORTUNITIES

The need for money to cover current expenses prevents many couples from placing some or more money in a savings account or an investment. Here is a way you can do so.

Many families have debts such as home mortgages, car loans and other obligations on which they make monthly payments.

The opportunity to save and invest money arises when the last payments are made on those obligations. Remind yourselves that while you have been making payments on those obligations, you also have been taking care of your other needs.

Don't let the money you have been paying each month on debts now slowly vanish by getting lost among other money needs that seem to always arise.

When a final payment soon will be made on a debt, plan for the amount of the payment to simultaneously move into a savings account or investment. Home mortgage loans and loans to purchase cars offer the most frequent opportunities. The end of any debt payments will give the same opportunity.

The same type of opportunity arises when you get a raise in your family income, a larger than expected bonus or receive an inheritance. Without a definite plan, the increased income *will slowly vanish.*

189

Many people borrow money to buy a new car, pay off that obligation and promptly go into debt again to buy another new car. Try to give yourselves some time between debt payments.

Going without a car debt payment for a year or two will be a great opportunity to start an investment plan that will be of great benefit to you over a period of time. Pay yourselves first and increase your family security!

Other great long-range savings opportunities are presented when you have *any* loan payments due every month. The procedure described in the "Housing" chapter for accelerating payments on your home mortgage can also be applied to payments on a car or other indebtedness.

The money saving idea presented is to pay an *additional amount* over and above the required monthly payment.

By doing so, you decrease the amount of interest you will otherwise pay in the long run. Most banks and other lending agencies will permit you to make additional or increased payments per month. Make sure, however, that the note you sign does not penalize you for doing so.

Review the accelerated payment chart in the "Housing" chapter to remind you of the savings you will achieve by increasing your monthly payment.

Extra payments on the principal will reduce the time required to pay off your loan. You will save money because your balance due will be lower and you will have less interest to pay.

190

PART IV
A LOOK AHEAD AT SPECIAL FEATURES OF THE MONEY MANAGEMENT SYSTEM

PART IV
A LOOK AHEAD AT SPECIAL FEATURES OF THE MONEY MANAGEMENT SYSTEM

At this point in the book you have been given an assortment of encouragements and challenges to develop a money management system. You have been given a wide range of information from several authors on subjects to prepare you for developing your system. You have also been given a wide range of suggestions on various topics on how you can spend your money more wisely. The time has come for you to develop your own money management system.

It has been demonstrated many times that a partial system on money management becomes no system. There is a temptation to develop part of a system with good intentions to complete it at a later date. We encourage you not to yield to that temptation.

The fact you are considering a money management system indicates you are having difficulty living within your income, or, if you are living within your income, you are not completely satisfied with the manner in which you are doing it.

As a prelude to developing your system, you need to give a great deal of consideration to all of the subjects where you feel you should do better in your planning and spending. The words "soul searching" might describe the mental process we are suggesting. Try to think of all of the things you could do more wisely.

We urge you to make a commitment to yourselves that you will stick with the project until you have completed it. Not halfway or three-quarters of the way, all the way! It will take a bit more time to do so, but you will be highly rewarded for your determination.

The No. 1 objective of this book on family money management is to make life better and easier for you.

At this time we are giving you a preview, and hopefully a pre-sell, of money management procedures we will be suggesting. We are explaining them now with the hope you will be ready to accept and use the procedures for your well-being and pleasure.

We are proposing greater use of multiple bank accounts and accrual accounts to make it easier for you to manage and monitor your expenses.

ACCRUAL TYPE ACCOUNTS

Our definition is that an accrual account is a scheduled setting aside of funds over a period of time in anticipation of a planned expenditure in the future. In a nutshell, that means having money *on hand* when you need it.

The subject of having accrual accounts might seem to be a new subject to you. It is highly probable, however, that you have had accrual accounts in the past without realizing it.

Most people have purchased a home or homes. They probably were financed with a mortgage on the home calling for a payment each month. That payment consisted of a payment on the mortgage plus money to be set aside to pay the real estate taxes and insurance premiums when due. That was an accrual account but probably not identified as such.

How would you have felt at the end of the year if no funds had been set aside to pay real estate taxes and insurance premiums and you suddenly realized you did not have the money available? Accrual accounts are designed to prevent that kind of unpleasant experience.

Through the years, accrual accounts have been understood and used by only a small percentage of individuals and families.

On the other hand, accrual accounts have been considered a necessity and used extensively by businesses. For example, a company with a fleet of trucks knows that when it buys a new truck there will come a time when they will need to replace it. If the company wants to continue in business, it needs to recognize the decline in value through use and depreciation, and set aside funds over a period of time. When the old truck wears out, the company has funds available to replace it.

Everyone knows that Christmas will be coming, and they will want to give presents to their family and close friends.

When it comes to paying for the presents there are two choices. You can plan ahead and set aside the money in advance so it will be available come December, or you can wait until December, buy the gifts and then worry how and when you are going to pay for them.

Vacations and mini-vacations throughout the year provide a similar example. You can plan ahead and set the money aside so it will be available when those occasions occur, or you can wait until the events and opportunities occur and then worry whether you can enjoy and pay for them.

Most family expenses repeat every month. A variety of expenses will not occur every month but will in the next few months, several months or year.

In this book we are trying to sell the idea that these expenses will be happy occasions if you plan in advance for the money. They will be stressful situations if you have to wonder and worry about the necessary money for important times in your lives.

HAVING MULTIPLE BANK ACCOUNTS

At first thought you might think that having several bank accounts would involve added work on your part. On the contrary — they will save you much time in your money management system.

You may have several charge accounts in different types of stores. When you opened those charge accounts, you probably had to fill out a form and give information. *If you can plan for the money involved, checking accounts are easier to establish than a charge account at a store.*

As you get acquainted with our suggested money management system, we hope you will be looking forward to bank accounts making your money management easier.

Our general money management plan is to have six management accounts. In those accounts you will develop your maximum spending goals and make allocations from your income available each month to provide the necessary money.

A great value of the bank accounts will mean a quick reading at the end of each month, by looking at the amount of money spent through your checking account and have an instant review on how you have done in relation to your goals for that management account.

There will be more information later on the benefits of multiple bank accounts in your money management system.

PART V
THE MONEY
MANAGEMENT SYSTEM

STEP ONE
GETTING ACQUAINTED WITH THE MASTER FORM — MONTHLY MONEY MANAGEMENT GOALS

Most of us have gone on trips. Taking a trip of any length requires planning. Where you want to go, how you plan to get there, what you need to take, etc. Planning how and where you want to spend your money is much the same. Planning is needed to ensure a happy journey. Life is a journey.

Your money management system starts with the Monthly Money Management Goals Form in Six Accounts To Make it Easier. We will refer to this as the Master Form.

The form could have been condensed into less space, but it is presented on five pages to give you ample spaces for writing in your numbers when it becomes timely to plan your financial future.

As we move into the establishment of your system your first question might be, "Where do we start?"

The answer is that developing a money management system might be likened to taking an automobile trip through several states. The first thing to do is to look at a map to learn all about the area.

In money management that means getting acquainted with all of the details of the system. In our case it is the Monthly Money Management Goals Form — the Master Form.

If you first looked at the *total* Master Form, you might have been overwhelmed at all of the accounts and categories. You might have thought, "This is complicated." We therefore present it one account at a time to make it easy to understand.

As you start working your way through the Master Form, all of the pieces will start fitting together. As you achieve completion of your system, we are confident you will say, "That wasn't too complicated."

Let's get acquainted step by step with the Master Form to learn what is involved.

If all of the action in a Money Management System were in one account, it would be very difficult to keep all of the subjects in mind.

It might, at first, seem that having six accounts would make your money management system more complicated. The opposite is true. The objective is to make your system as simple as possible. It would be overwhelming to have many details in just one account. We have, therefore, followed the old military maxim, "Divide and conquer." Having six accounts allows you to plan and see, at a glance, where your money is going.

We will frequently be referring in the text to management accounts, bank accounts, accrual accounts and categories. When we mention a subject *generally*, such as accrual accounts, it will not be capitalized. If we mention a *specific* account, such as the No. 1 Main Accrual Account, it will be capitalized. We hope the distinctions will be helpful to you.

In presenting the Master Form we start with the Summary of Income and Summary of Planned Use.

SUMMARY OF INCOME
INCOME:
Average Monthly Income $_____
Other Income $_____
Total Income $_____
Optional Reserve for Inadequate Planning or Overspending $_____
Balance Available: To Be Distributed To Accounts Through the Bank Account for the No. 6 General Account $_____

SUMMARY OF PLANNED USE	
DISTRIBUTION TO ACCOUNTS:	$_____
1. Family Security Account	$_____
2. Main Accrual Account	$_____
3. Christmas and Gift Account	$_____
4. Vacation Account	$_____
5. Household Account	$_____
6. General Account	$_____
TOTAL	$_____
Needs To Be Even With or Below **Balance Available**	

This is the part of the form that will help you identify the amount of money you have available for spending for an account in an average month.

At this time, give attention to the top half of the form.

The "income" part of the form provides space for the total average income per month and any "other income" expected each month. The total should be the amount you *know* you can depend on receiving *every* month. Bonuses or occasional extra income should not be considered in this total.

If your monthly income varies, we suggest you use an average of the lowest estimated amounts in your planning. If your income is sometimes higher, there will always be places where you can use the excess.

Some comments on your Summary of Income might be helpful. Try hard to develop solid figures on what your income will be.

Some people apparently claim fewer tax exemptions on the W-4s than realistic in the hope of receiving a tax refund. We suggest that you do not use this type of money management.

We recommend generally that a bonus not be considered as income until it actually becomes income. If the bonus income is on a solid and predictable formula, a small *part* of the bonus *might* be considered as income on a conservative basis. When the total amount of the bonus is paid, any excess over the conservative amount used should be placed in the Family Security Account presented later.

For a parent or parents on low income who qualify for earned income credit at tax filing time, 60 percent of the qualified amount can be paid by the employer, prorated over the year, by completing and submitting a W-5 to the employer. This can increase monthly income by as much as $150.

We have provided a space for an Optional Reserve if you wish to protect yourselves against insufficient planning or overspending in the early stages of perfecting your system.

As you review the amount of your income and your planned expenditures, it would be great if you could plan your expenditures and your follow-through so well that you can meet exact amounts. That is difficult, especially in the first few months of getting your money management system under way. If you are confident you can meet your goals and control your expenses, you do not need a reserve for insufficient planning or overspending. If you do not have that strong confidence in establishing and meeting your spending goals, we recommend that you establish an Optional Reserve to cover mistakes in planning or overspending in the early months of your new management plan. Do as you think necessary in your situation. One possible solution is to set aside an amount less than 10 percent of your income to cover planning mistakes or overspending. This reserve should not be necessary for more than a few months.

To complete this part of the planning process, total all of the monthly income, subtract an Optional Reserve if you wish, and enter the total of the Balance Available to distribute to the six accounts. This total reflects how much money you have available each month for expenses.

If you have additional income from time to time, we will suggest later how you might use those funds.

The totals on the lower half of the page of the *Summary of Planned Use* will need to be filled in later after you determine what you plan to allocate and spend through each of the accounts. There will be categories in each account to help you determine the total needed for each account.

The amounts to be spent through the accounts will be determined when you develop your maximum expense goal for each category in each account. That will involve deciding how you want your money to be spent.

We now present the No. 1 Family Security Account.

<table>
<tr><td colspan="2"><u>NO. 1 – FAMILY SECURITY ACCOUNT</u></td></tr>
<tr><td>SAVINGS ACCOUNT – Deposit each month</td><td>$_____</td></tr>
<tr><td>MEDICAL and DENTAL RESERVE – Deposit each month. If you do not have full health insurance, and only partial or no coverage, you, in effect, become a self-insurer. It is necessary to deposit money each month to be prepared for these expenses. You have to set aside money to take care of the expenses or the deductible involved.</td><td>$_____</td></tr>
<tr><td>INVESTMENT – To be made each month</td><td>$_____</td></tr>
<tr><td>INSURANCE PREMIUMS
Insurance in its many forms is an important part of family security. <u>Monthly</u> premiums are paid from the General Account. <u>Other</u> premiums are paid from the Main Accrual Account so a monthly deposit needs to be made to that Account to cover those expenses when they develop.</td><td></td></tr>
<tr><td>TOTAL MONTHLY DEPOSITS TO BE MADE</td><td>$_____</td></tr>
</table>

Professional counselors on family money management have long recommended that people should "pay yourself first" to provide security for the family.

This starts with establishing a savings account and depositing money into it *every month*. Think of the monthly deposit as a firm commitment, not as something you may or may not do every month. It also calls for setting aside money to pay medical and dental expenses not covered by insurance. With or without insurance, you must set aside enough money to pay all of those "bound-to-come — sooner or later" medical expenses.

205

Most financial counselors suggest that a family should have enough cash or assets easily convertible to cash to carry the family for six months if health problems or any unexpected situations develop. That may seem impossible to you at this point, but work toward that goal of a six-month safety net. If the family security account is not placed first in your planning, it probably will never be given the priority it deserves.

There is nothing more important to a family than the feeling of *security*, and there are levels of security for every family. The word "security" can mean many things. Will we have money to see a doctor if we get sick? Will we have food so we won't be hungry? Will we have the necessary clothes? Can we keep warm in the winter? Can we live normal happy lives? Will we live in fear there is something missing in our lives? Family security *is important*, and it starts with this account.

Even for a family with other money to back them, some money should be invested in a savings account where funds will be readily available. After that fund is soundly established, excess funds can be put into long-term investments. There are many qualified advisors who can assist you when you reach that stage.

As a prelude to the presentation of the three accrual accounts, we think it will be helpful to you to have some further explanations of those important accounts.

The Main Accrual Account will have to be planned first. There is *much less discretion* on the expenses that will have to be paid from that account.

For example, there is no discretion on items like real estate taxes to be paid at the end of the year (unless they are set aside as part of your mortgage payments), insurance premiums on policies annually or semi-annually, debt payments that must be met on a due date or automobile taxes and license fees that probably have to be paid in a certain month.

There is more discretion in the Christmas and Gift and the Vacation Accounts. These accounts, however, have very strong need for family security and happiness.

The total amount needed for a year in an accrual account will be easy to calculate. You can enter on the form the amount that will be needed in specific months under each of the subjects. The total for these amounts divided by twelve will give you the *average* monthly amount that needs to be deposited in that accrual bank account.

It is suggested you plan your accrual accounts *well in advance* so the average monthly deposit will be adequate. If your disbursement for a certain subject has to be paid in a few months, it would be necessary to increase the amount of your monthly deposits in order to be ready.

As you start to plan your accrual accounts, you first need to plan how much money you need or wish to set aside each month that will later be disbursed through those accounts. The total amount available for all accounts will be your average monthly income minus your average monthly living expenses. If it develops you do not have sufficient funds to cover all of your desires and expenses, first cut as much as possible on other items before cutting any allocations to accrual accounts. Read those important guidelines again.

Here is another reminder of the value of accrual accounts. If you are going to make purchases, you have two choices. You can save the money in advance and have the cash ready, or you can go into debt when you make the purchases and then wonder how you are going to pay for them. That would generally mean going into debt for a few months or more on a credit card debt, a department store charge account on which you pay interest, or a bank loan.

It would be appropriate to describe the No. 2, No. 3 and No. 4 accrual accounts as "peace of mind" accounts because they will provide just that.

We are calling the No. 2 Main Accrual Account the first accrual account because it covers several subjects on which there is little or no flexibility for setting money aside in advance to cover several subjects.

Real estate and other taxes, insurance premiums, automobile taxes and registrations must be paid on time so there is no discretion involved as to amounts or dates of payment. We have thus placed the No. 2 Main Accrual Account as the first accrual account. There is more discretion on the amounts set aside in the No. 3 Christmas and Gift Account and the No. 4 Vacation Account.

As indicated above, it is highly desirable that all of the accrual accounts be started in your plan on day one. Only if your financial affairs need more time should there be any delay in establishing the accounts. Sooner or later, your spending will have to be brought under control to produce the money to be set aside in the accrual accounts so try very hard to do it at the beginning rather than later.

We now present the No. 2 Main Accrual Account.

NO. 2 – MAIN ACCRUAL ACCOUNT

This is designed for money to be set aside to be expended later for expenses that are not paid every month. Enter the amount you will need to pay in a specific month. Use an additional page if necessary.

CATEGORY	Insurance Premiums not Paid Monthly	Annual Taxes (Home, Car)	Other	MONTHLY TOTAL
January				
February				
March				
April				
May				
June				
July				
August				
September				
October				
November				
December				
TOTALS				

YEARLY GRAND TOTAL $_____   MONTHLY AVERAGE $_____
(Monthly Deposit Required)

Enter these amounts for later monitoring.

Amount Needed in Next Three Months $_____	Amount Needed in Next Six Months $_____	Amount Needed in Balance of Year $_____

This account will be used on a wider assortment of subjects than the following Christmas
and Gift and Vacation Accounts.

Examples for this account are insurance premiums not paid monthly, real estate taxes, car
taxes and licenses and other expenses that recur
every year.

This account can be called the first "peace of
mind" account because it helps you set aside
money in advance so when an amount is due you
have the money available. It will take time and
study, but you will be highly rewarded for your
efforts.

If possible, pay your insurance premiums and
other obligations monthly. On insurance premiums and other expenses that are not paid monthly, place the funds in the Main Accrual Account
so they will be available when the money is due.

In a column of the form, identify the subject and
the amount you will need to pay in the month it is
due. Use separate columns on the form to add
other subjects. Total the figures for each month and
add the 12 months together for a 12-month total.

Taking the 12-month total and dividing it by
12 will give you the monthly *average* amount
you need to set aside.

In the Family Security Account we suggested a
savings account to be used primarily for emer-
gencies. *That suggestion stands.*

The Main Accrual Account was designed for identified expenditures. You may need to make an additional page or two of the form.

There probably will come a time or times when you want to add an expense to be paid through your Main Accrual Account.

Each new subject added would generally call for an additional deposit to be made to the account each month.

A good alternative would be to add an *extra amount* over and above your *needed* average monthly deposit to set up a reserve to take care of new subjects that might arise. This might be described as a *"working* savings account" to provide some money and remove the temptation to take it from your Family Security Account.

If you do not have the "working savings account," an added desired expenditure might be handled in the following way: Determine the amount of the added expenditure you desire and the number of months you have to accumulate the money. Calculate the average monthly amount needed and add it to the bank account for your Main Accrual Account. The money then will be there when you need it.

You will need to monitor your accrual accounts each month to make sure you are accumulating enough money to cover expenditures coming up. There will be a complete guide on this monitoring in Step Three — The "Follow-

Through" — Checking Your Progress In Achieving Your Goals.

We now present the No. 3 Christmas and Gift Account.

NO. 3 – CHRISTMAS AND GIFT ACCOUNT					
Enter the maximum amount you plan to <u>spend</u> in each month.					
CATEGORY	Christmas	Anniv.	Birthdays	Other	MONTHLY TOTAL
January					
February					
March					
April					
May					
June					
July					
August					
September					
October					
November					
December					
TOTALS					
YEARLY GRAND TOTAL $_____ MONTHLY AVERAGE $_____ (Monthly Deposit Required)					
Enter these amounts for later monitoring.					
Amount Needed in Next Three Months $_____		Amount Needed in Next Six Months $_____		Amount Needed in Balance of Year $_____	

This is a relatively simple accrual account to give you more pleasure at Christmas and other gift-giving times. It is an account that serves the specific purposes of having money set aside to cover those expenses.

Gift giving is important. Not planning ahead causes pressure and may create one crisis after another. Consider all of the times throughout the year that you want to purchase gifts, both large and small. List the amounts you wish to spend, by month, on this form. Because of shortage of funds, you may have to start this account with low amounts and increase them when you can. But do *start* this account now!

Taking the yearly total and dividing by 12 will give you the monthly average you need to deposit in that account.

Counting the months between now and year's end and multiplying that number by the monthly average deposit will tell you if you have sufficient funds for the balance of the year. If not, you can plan and act accordingly.

With Christmas falling at the end of the year, the ideal time to start this account is December 1, *twelve months ahead* of the December in which most of your presents will be purchased. If you start this account late in the year you will need higher than average monthly deposits to be ready.

Next is the No. 4 Vacation Account.

CATEGORY	Main Vacation	Mini Vacation	MONTHLY TOTAL
NO. 4 – VACATION ACCOUNT			
Enter the maximum amount you plan to spend each month.			
January			
February			
March			
April			
May			
June			
July			
August			
September			
October			
November			
December			
TOTALS			

YEARLY GRAND TOTAL $_____   MONTHLY AVERAGE $_____
(Monthly Deposit Required)

Enter these amounts for later monitoring.

Amount Needed in Next Three Months $_____   Amount Needed in Next Six Months $_____   Amount Needed in Balance of Year $_____

Family vacations can be times of building treasured memories of family times together. They may involve a main vacation plus special days or hours of "mini-vacations."

Vacations are an important time for building family relationships and renewal. They should be a priority for every family. We repeat a suggestion from the No. 3 Account. Because of shortage of funds, you may have to start this account with low amounts and increase them when you can, but start this account now.

If money is short, vacations can be spent at home, just doing some special things together with minimal expenses, like fishing, or other leisure activity. Planning ahead can make vacations a relaxing and enjoyable time. The ideal time to start this account is at least 12 months before your main vacation plus ample time before the first mini-vacation.

Dollars are important, but treasured memories of family times together are far more important. Those times together might be labeled vacations, mini-vacations, times together or not have a "label" — but they are very important to the lives of everyone. *Plan them!*

The Household Account on page 217 will use an important percentage of your monthly spendable income. It covers a variety of daily, weekly and monthly expenses that most families have.

Account No. 5 is the Household Account.

NO. 5 – HOUSEHOLD ACCOUNT		
Enter the Maximum Expense Goal you plan to spend in the coming month in each Category. The figures will probably vary only slightly from month to month.		
EXPENSE CATEGORIES		
Groceries	$_____	$_____
Meals Out	$_____	$_____
Utilities	$_____	$_____
Phone, Television, etc	$_____	$_____
Laundry/Dry Cleaning	$_____	$_____
Drugs and Toiletries	$_____	$_____
Sitters and Household Help	$_____	$_____
Child Care	$_____	$_____
Wife's Clothes	$_____	$_____
Children's Clothes	$_____	$_____
School	$_____	$_____
Car Payment	$_____	$_____
Car Expenses	$_____	$_____
Club Dues and Hobbies	$_____	$_____
Children's Allowances	$_____	$_____
Petty Cash	$_____	$_____
	TOTAL	$_____

217

There are spaces for you to add additional categories, as needed, by your family.

On this form you will be recording your very important maximum spending goals for each category.

Because this account covers so many different categories, it will take time to complete. Do take the time necessary to give it your very best efforts.

Once you think you have listed everything, go back through your checkbook, paid bills and recollections covering three months to see if there is anything you may have forgotten that will help you establish a sound goal for each category. Also review carefully your out-of-pocket expenses for the past three months.

The last account on the Master Form is the No. 6 General Account.

In addition to the categories of expenses in this General Account, it will also be used to accumulate your monthly income and distribute it to the six accounts in your management system.

NO. 6 – GENERAL ACCOUNT

Enter the Maximum Expense Goals you plan to spend in the coming month in each Category. The figures will probably vary only slightly from month to month.

EXPENSE CATEGORIES		EXPENSE CATEGORIES	
Rent/House Payment	$____	Insurance	
		Home	$____
Car Payment	$____		
		Automobile	
Car Expenses	$____	(Husband & Wife)	$____
Other Debt Payments	$____	Life	$____
		Disability	$____
Clothes	$____		
		Medical	$____
Club Dues and Hobbies	$____		$____
Contributions	$____	**ALLOCATIONS TO OTHER ACCOUNTS**	
Petty Cash	$____		
	$____	No. 1 Family Security Account	$____
____	$____	No. 2 Main Account	$____
____	$____	No. 3 Christmas and Gift Account	$____
____	$____	No. 4 Vacation Account	$____
____	$____	No. 5 Household Account	$____
____	$____	No. 6 General Account	$____
		TOTAL	$____

You can customize this form to meet the needs of your family by adding categories, if needed.

If you have *several* different expenses that fall into *one* of the listed categories, you may want to list each in a separate category to make it easier for you to develop your category goals and monitor your performance.

219

The general objective of the No. 2 Main Accrual Account is to plan and set aside money for the specific items set forth on the form. This accrual account also can be used as a "working savings account" to cover expenses that will be occurring in the future that are hard to identify from the standpoint of the amount, the nature of the expense or when it might happen. Examples would be home or automobile maintenance. Those expenses will be occurring in the future, but the nature and timing of the expenses cannot be predicted.

A good plan would be to deposit in this account each month something more than those that are easy to predict. This additional amount can be used when these expenses do arise. Having some extra funds in this account would eliminate the temptation to take money out of the Family Security Account for this purpose.

In the No. 5 Household Account and the No. 6 General Account, there are spaces for the amount to be spent in an average month for clothing. The clothing will not be purchased every month, so some provision has to be made to set aside money for the months for which the clothing will be purchased. That money might be maintained in the No. 5 Household Account or No. 6 General Account, but it might also be placed in the No. 2 Main Accrual Account to be available when necessary.

Household and automobile maintenance expenses might be treated in the same way as clothing by being maintained in the Household or General Accounts or being placed in the Main Accrual Account.

These amounts might be retained in the No. 5 Household or No. 6 General Account, but we suggest you consider putting the funds in the No. 2 Main Accrual Account. The important point is that you put those amounts aside and not let those funds be dissipated for other purposes.

The more accurate and realistic your maximum spending goals figures are, the easier it will be for you in making your money management system work smoothly. It will also make the monitoring of your expenses easier when you get to the "follow-through" stage explained in a later chapter.

A complete family money management system should be started at one time but may not be completed at that time. It will help if you realize that it will take patience and determination.

A complete plan is presented here and is the ultimate objective.

The No. 5 Household Account and No. 6 General Account should be started and completed first.

The No. 2 Main Accrual Account, No. 3 Christmas and Gift Account and No. 4 Vacation

Account should be started, if only on a modest scale. The No. 2 Account will take priority because you have less choice about meeting obligations like taxes than those in the No. 3 and No. 4 Accounts that involve discretionary expenses.

You will be studying what you have been spending on each category in the past. This will put you on your way to establishing your maximum spending goals for each category. At this time, however, do not enter any figures on the Master Form.

The establishment of all maximum spending goals should be the joint responsibility of the adults in the household, with the children becoming involved where appropriate.

With all adults and wage earners involved in developing all maximum spending goals, it will set the stage for a monthly review on how things are going.

Communication among family members will be very important in checking how the system is working. Everyone should become involved in the monthly progress review.

A longtime consultant in the field of money management for families feels the monthly progress review meetings are a great influence in family cooperation and harmony. The objective of these meetings should be to cooperate and help each other rather than to find opportunities for criticizing.

In the next stage of developing your money management system, you will need many copies of the pages of the master form in developing your maximum spending goals in the various accounts and categories.

We suggest you have the pages of the Master Form enlarged to approximately 8 $^1/_2$ by 11 inches for ease in writing your numbers. Start with at least 10 copies of each of the pages of the Master Form. Visit your favorite copy shop soon and get ready!

STEP TWO
DEVELOPING FIGURES FROM
THE PAST AND PLANNING YOUR
MAXIMUM SPENDING GOALS

A French philosopher might have been thinking about money management when he said, *"There is only one reason to look back and that is to get a direction for the future."*

Developing information from the past and planning maximum spending goals in each account and category may be the most time-consuming task in developing your money management system. The time spent also will be the most rewarding.

You probably will have to give your patience and determination several boosts along the way.

The better the job you do in establishing your *maximum spending goal* for each category, the easier it will be in monitoring your progress later.

In money management there are many reasons to look back. Doing so can help you develop the information and figures that will help chart your course for the future. Facts and experience from the past serve as a foundation upon which to build a solid financial plan.

There are several ways you can develop this type of information. If you have been paying for many of your expenses by check, credit card, charge accounts or paying cash and getting receipts, that information will be very helpful and a good beginning.

If you don't have this type of information from the past, you will need to *estimate*, as carefully as possible, the amounts you have been or plan to be spending in an average month for *each category* on the form.

Do your best on these estimates. This is not a time for "wishful thinking." This is a time for realities. The more accurate your estimates, the less you will have to adjust the total of your accounts and goals to meet your monthly balance available.

Each family may have expenses not listed on the form. It is important you add categories, if necessary, to the form to fit your planning needs.

The first step as you move forward in building your new plan is to look at what you *have* been spending or plan to limit that spending in *each* of the categories under *each* account.

Place the goal amounts on each category line in the various accounts. If you have not been spending anything for that category, place a zero on the line. If you have exact figures, place those amounts in the appropriate spaces. If it is an estimate, do your estimating as carefully as possible and put the estimate on the proper line.

Some items, like clothing, might be purchased in only three or four months of the year, but the

225

money for clothing and similar expenses has to be planned each month. This will ensure the monthly funds are spent or held wisely for purchases later.

The solution for this situation is to plan the *average* amount for each month even though it is not spent in every month. This is a situation that may not justify a separate accrual account but does require planning. As stated previously, the No. 2 Main Accrual Account might be used for clothing.

You need to use all pages of the Master Form as you start to build your plan. It is probable the figures will go through several changes, so have several copies of the Master Form available.

In time, you will probably have figures in each category in each account on the form. Some may be exact and some may be "best estimates," or a combination of past history and estimates for the future.

After you have figures in every account and category, you can total the figures for *each* account. The next step is to total the figures for *all* six accounts for a grand total.

Compare the grand total of these figures to your *Balance Available to be Distributed to Accounts* in the top space on the first page of the Master Form.

Then you will have a peek at the challenges you might be facing. The odds are that your spending goals will exceed your balance available. If so, go back through the form and reduce or increase your goals in each account and category, as needed.

You will have to make decisions on which accounts and categories to change in order to come within your balance available.

As you work your way through the planning process, it is probable many expenses that you thought were *"essential"* — *needs* — will have to be moved into the *"discretionary"* — *wants* — classification.

As you put your first figures together and get your first grand total for all accounts, you might feel you can't cut your expenses enough to meet your balance available. That will be tough, but it will prove that you need to get with a sound management plan.

If you have been spending too much money in the past and need to cut some expenses, you probably will benefit from the real-life expense control experience of two partners in a business where expenses were too high.

One of the partners was young and with little experience. The other partner was older and with much experience. When it became apparent expenses were too high, the young partner said, "We have to make *big* cuts in a *couple* of our expenses." The older partner said, "No, we are not going to get our expenses in line by cutting a *couple* of expenses *a lot*. We need to cut *a lot* of expenses a little." So it is with family financial planning.

Very few individuals or families have developed a perfect plan on their first or even their second or third try. Do the best you can, but be prepared for many adjustments. That is the nature of the project.

At some point you will be tempted to put an amount here or there that will bring your total for all accounts down to your balance available. *Resist the temptation and keep working* to develop *solid* figures with which you know you can live.

There will probably be many trial and error estimates leading to final figures on the many accounts and categories of the master form. Just keep reminding yourselves that the final result will be well worth your efforts.

It was reported that the first inaugural address of President Franklin D. Roosevelt went through nine revisions before it was in final form. In the ninth revision, only one word was changed. Anticipate that your total planning process will go through many revisions before you can say with confidence, "That's it."

Now, you are ready for the "follow-through!"

STEP THREE
THE "FOLLOW-THROUGH" — CHECKING YOUR PROGRESS IN ACHIEVING YOUR GOALS

If you are a golfer or have been around golfers, you have heard about the importance of the "follow-through."

In golf, you swing the club to the ball. Stopping the club-head at that point would result in moving the ball only a few feet. That is not enough. To achieve the maximum result, you have to continue your swing and *effort all the way.* It is the same way in family money management. *That* is the "follow-through."

If you have done a good job of developing figures on your past spending — studied them — put your final maximum spending goals in the categories on the Master Form — you are ready for *your* "follow-through."

The "follow-through" involves making sure you are keeping your expenditures under control and thus meeting your objectives.

We want you to do it with the least amount of work on your part, consistent with a *solid* "follow-through."

USING BANK ACCOUNTS TO HELP YOU CHECK YOUR PROGRESS

It is recommended you have a bank account to go with each of your management accounts. You might ask, "Do we need up to six bank accounts?"

A short and quick answer might be, "If you want peace of mind, the bank accounts will give it to you." A longer answer would be:

1. To help you keep track of your money and expenditures so you have confidence in your money management system.

2. To keep you from mixing all of your expenses and funds in one account. Mixing funds in one account might result in your spending money for some things that will later leave you without money needed for other things that are very important.

3. To help you do a better and easier job of planning and spending your money.

As stated before, one of the most important objectives of this book is to provide a money management system that will be easy to master with the least amount of work on your part.

Our first suggestion has been that you have a bank account to go with each of your money management accounts.

If you are doing a fairly good job of living within your income, the bank accounts probably will provide all of the monitoring you need.

At the *beginning* of each month, place in the bank account for each of the management accounts the maximum amount you planned to *accrue* in the accrual accounts and *spend* in the other accounts.

At the end of the month, when you get your bank statement for each account, you can compare the amounts you accrued and spent through the accrual accounts and the amounts you spent through the other accounts compared to the allocations to the accounts.

If you have kept your spending within the total for all of the categories in the account, you will see that you have kept your expenditures in line.

You might have to double check to make sure your *total* expenditures looked good only because you *underspent* in some of the categories.

If your expenditures were in excess of the total for the account, it will be a sign you need to adjust your spending downward in some categories.

If you spent more money in an account in a month than you had planned to spend, you will need to check each category in the account to see where you overspent.

It then may be necessary to revise your category goals, upward or downward, for the following month.

If the amount involved is not too large, you can do a bit of planning and still use the bank account as your monitoring system.

If your expenditures were far over your total goal for the account, you may need to use the goals monitoring procedure described a bit later. Try first, however, to make your bank account monitoring system achieve your objectives. Don't do any more work than necessary.

The next step will be for you to place in that bank account the revised amount you plan to spend from the account in the following month.

The grand total for all accounts must continue to be within the total amount available.

Your objective is to keep all of your expenses in line with the least amount of monitoring on your part. If your living expenses are *comfortable* in relation to your income, the bank accounts generally will give you assurance your system is working properly. You will be pleased your bank accounts are producing your "follow-through" with little work by you.

MONITORING YOUR ACCRUAL ACCOUNTS

There is a great benefit from having a bank account to go with each of the *accrual* accounts. You can see at a glance whether you have sufficient funds in those bank accounts to cover the expenditures coming up.

The first step in this monitoring process started on the bottom of each accrual account. Hopefully, you entered on the bottom of *each* of the accrual accounts the total of the expenditures scheduled in the next three months, six months and year.

The next step is to compare the balance in each bank account with the amounts needed for the expenditures coming up.

If the funds are adequate, you don't have to do anything until you check again next month.

If the bank account is short of the amount needed, you will have to add funds to the bank account in time to be ready for the expenditures. You also will have to make certain, if necessary, that you adjust your spending downward to get within the money available.

Don't let the number of bank accounts worry you. When we mention six bank accounts, we are thinking of two active accounts, the No. 5 Household Account and No. 6 General Account. The other four accounts will have limited activity as savings or checking accounts — the No. 1 Family Security Account, No. 2 Main Accrual Account, No. 3 Christmas and Gift Account and No. 4 Vacation Account.

You *could* use just one bank account, but that would require you to maintain six *monthly money management accounts* in *one bank account.* That would take hours of *your* time in tracking how much money you *need* against what you *have* available for each of the accounts.

The easy way to monitor your accounts and category goals is to have a *bank* account for *each* of your six *management* accounts.

As you get into the follow-through process, you will realize the bank accounts will *simplify* your money management system.

Think in terms of letting a bank or banks make your follow-through much easier.

As you study the details, you will realize there will be very little activity in your *management* Family Security Account and *bank* Family Security Account. This savings account will have one or two deposits per month and, hopefully, few withdrawals over a long period.

There will be some activity in your *management* Main Accrual Account and your *bank* Main Accrual Account. There should be limited activity in your *management* Christmas and Gift Account and *bank* Christmas and Gift Account.

You will make only one or two deposits per month and probably average less than one withdrawal from the Christmas and Gift bank account in an average month.

The same will be true in your *management* Vacation Account and your *bank* Vacation Account.

We have suggested three accrual accounts that we feel will best serve most families. You might wish to merge one or two of your accrual accounts, but do so only after very careful consideration. Make certain that any change that you consider is a sound approach for you that will improve your total plan. Stay with the procedure unless you are certain you have a better way to serve your needs. Too many changes will result in no plan at all.

With very little bank account activity, there should not be any bank account service charges, or very small ones, on these four bank accounts.

We *do not* recommend it, but if having six bank accounts is a concern, you *might carefully* consider combining some bank accounts as you get your money management system under way.

The *bank* Main Accrual Account might be combined with your *bank* Christmas and Gift and bank Vacation Accounts. They all have the same purpose of setting money aside that will be needed for specific purposes in the months ahead.

The *bank* Family Security Account should only receive deposits and then grow with interest earned and be available when emergency funds are needed. Out of a total of six accounts that would leave only two additional bank accounts — one each for the more active *General* and *Household* Accounts.

The difficulties of co-mingling your money in one bank account are easy to understand. You are encouraged to have six bank accounts, but you *might* get by with less.

You would have to do more work yourselves to keep track of your management system accounts if you have only one bank account. Your work would be to personally provide the controls and record keeping the bank accounts would otherwise provide you. A few dollars per month in bank service charges would save much time for you and *be money well spent.*

With only *one* bank account, *you* would have to make sure you keep the funds separated for *each* of your six money management accounts. If money that was intended for a specific use is used for something else, your system might get wrecked.

The biggest factor in favor of six bank accounts is that setting money aside for specific needs will prevent that money from getting into one bank account from which it can easily *"get lost"* and *disappear.* Again, think in terms of the bank or banks doing your money management paperwork for you.

Most of the bank account activity will be in the General and Household Accounts. There will be very limited activity in the bank accounts of the Family Security Account, the Main Accrual Account, Christmas and Gift Account and Vacation Account.

If it is too difficult to open six accounts, you might start with just two accounts, the General and the Household. You then can move the money out of those accounts to the other accounts as you build up funds.

You might have one or two of the accounts in one bank and one or two in other banks, savings and loans or credit unions.

As you start to get your money management system under way, it will be wise to visit with a bank or banks and get their suggestions on the best accounts for you. That means choosing accounts that will meet your needs with the lowest possible monthly service charges.

It may be desirable to have the names of both spouses on each bank account with only one signature being required on a check. You might have a *General* Account, John and Mary Doe; *Household* Account, John and Mary Doe; etc. These are just examples.

On the other hand, some families may need to recognize that one of the spouses has a weakness for writing checks on any account available. If that situation exists, the person with that inclination should restrict himself/herself to the account covering expenses for which only he/she is responsible.

Although there may be some fees involved in maintaining your bank accounts, they will produce great benefits for you and your family. This system will also save you valuable time you might prefer to spend on leisure or other activities.

To help your "follow-through" and for your record-keeping purposes, it is suggested you *pay for grocery and other major expenses by check, debit card, credit card or charge account payable during or at the end of the month.*

If you do write checks, be mindful that it is *money* that comes right out of your bank account. Whether you spend money by check or cash, be aware it is *money* and hopefully money being wisely spent.

Banks sometimes will issue two or more credit cards to a person or couple who use the cards for different purposes. You might get a separate card to be used only for "Groceries" and one for "Meals Out" or another category where there are a number of expenditures in a month.

At the end of the month, with the use of a credit card or debit card, the total for each category of expenditures can be easily compared to your category goal.

If you do use credit cards for this purpose, it would be important to make sure the credit cards are used for no other purposes. If you want to compare the expenditures to a category goal, always make sure the credit cards are *paid in full each month.*

Using credit cards for any purpose is recommended only when the total balance is paid each month. Bear in mind there may be annual charges to secure each credit card. These charges hopefully will be reasonable compared to the record-keeping time you would otherwise have to personally spend.

You might have a service station credit card or charge account for the gas and oil category. The caution remains that such an account be paid in full every month.

There will be some expenses for which cash payments will have to be made. If so, get all possible receipts to help you record what you spend compared to your category goals.

There will be expenses for which cash is usually paid and getting receipts is inconvenient. *Be mindful that having cash in your pocket or purse provides temptations to let money slip through your fingers.*

Finally, you have to make certain your accrual accounts are working properly. Each month you need to review each of the four accrual *bank* accounts to determine that each bank account has a sufficient balance to cover the planned expenditures in the next three months, six months or balance of the year.

If no withdrawals have been made from the family security and accrual accounts in a month, you still need to be sure regular monthly deposits are being made.

On the accrual accounts, make sure every month that the balances remaining, plus your future monthly deposits, will be sufficient to replenish the accounts to the desired levels for expenditures in the coming months. You will have to increase your monthly deposits if you have made expenditures not previously planned.

On your accrual accounts, a monthly review of the current bank balances, minus your expected withdrawals, plus your planned deposits during the next three or more months, will quickly tell you if your monthly deposit to any account needs to be immediately increased.

Following is a review of using bank accounts to monitor your performance.

A REVIEW — TEN IMPORTANT STEPS EACH MONTH IN MONITORING YOUR EXPENSES

FOR THE NO. 5 HOUSEHOLD ACCOUNT AND NO. 6 GENERAL ACCOUNT WITH A BANK ACCOUNT FOR EACH

1. Each month, very carefully prepare your total maximum spending goals for all categories in the No. 5 Household Account and No. 6 General Account and have a bank account for each account.

2. Make sure the total planned allocations and expenditures through these accounts, plus the other four system accounts, are not in excess of the monthly amount available.

3. Allocate and deposit the amounts in the bank accounts for each of the six management accounts.

4. Maintain a deposit and check register for each of the bank accounts, particularly for the No. 5 Household Account and No. 6 General Account. Be mindful of the current balance and the percent of the total expenditures to date, in relation to the total monthly goal for that management account.

241

5. If necessary, about mid-month start verifying your check register balance with the bank's record of your balance for each account.

6. If necessary, increase this verification toward the end of the month to protect against overdrafts. Don't write any checks unless you are certain you have the funds in the bank.

7. Toward the end of the month, compare your bank account balance to your management account goals and review how you are doing.

8. Where necessary, adjust your management account goals for the coming month. Once again, verify that the total for all accounts is within your amount available for spending.

9. Revise, if necessary, your allocations and deposits for the coming month, and repeat your monthly monitoring procedure.

10. Profit from your experiences and improve each month. After a few months, you will need few changes.

The above reminders particularly relate to the No. 5 Household Account and No. 6 General Account.

Don't forget, however the additional reminders of the importance of monitoring the Nos. 1, 2, 3 and 4 Accounts.

MORE DETAILED EXPENSE MONITORING — THE GOALS MONITORING PROCEDURE

In relation to your Money Management System, "monitoring" is defined as providing "a reminder or warning when financial management needs greater control."

As indicated previously, it is recognized that some individuals and families will need more category monitoring than is provided by the bank account method. For that purpose we present our Goals Monitoring Procedure.

The bank account method provides an overview on how you are doing in each *management account.* The Goals Monitoring Procedure provides more *detailed* monitoring of expenses in selected categories, particularly in the No. 5 Household Account and No. 6 General Account.

The Goals Monitoring System is on the following four pages. Form No. 1 covers the Family Security Account. Form No. 2 covers the three accrual accounts. Form No. 3 is designed to assist you in monitoring the expense categories in the Household Account, and Form No. 4 will help you keep track of the expenses in the General Account where you might have difficulty in keeping your expenses within some of your category goals.

GOALS MONITORING FORM NO. 1

Record dates and entries for a reading compared to Goals.

FAMILY SECURITY ACCOUNT

SAVINGS ACCOUNT		INVESTMENT ACCOUNT	
BEGINNING BALANCE		BEGINNING BALANCE	
MONTHLY DEPOSIT GOAL		MONTHLY DEPOSIT GOAL	
DATE DEPOSIT		DATE DEPOSIT	
DATE DEPOSIT		DATE DEPOSIT	
TOTAL DEPOSITS		TOTAL DEPOSITS	
DATE WITHDRAWL		DATE WITHDRAWL	
ENDING BALANCE		GAINS (LOSSES)	
INTEREST EARNED		TOTAL	
TOTAL		SAVINGS ACCOUNT TOTAL	
		GRAND TOTAL	

GOALS MONITORING FORM NO. 2

Record dates and entries for a reading compared to Goals.

MAIN ACCRUAL ACCOUNT, CHRISTMAS AND GIFT ACCRUAL ACCOUNT, VACATION ACCRUAL ACCOUNT

MAIN ACCRUAL ACCOUNT		CHRISTMAS AND GIFT ACCRUAL ACCOUNT		VACATION ACCRUAL ACCOUNT	
BEGINNING BALANCE		BEGINNING BALANCE		BEGINNING BALANCE	
MONTHLY DEPOSIT GOAL		MONTHLY DEPOSIT GOAL		MONTHLY DEPOSIT GOAL	
DATE DEPOSIT		DATE DEPOSIT		DATE DEPOSIT	
DATE DEPOSIT		DATE DEPOSIT		DATE DEPOSIT	
TOTAL DEPOSITS		TOTAL DEPOSITS		TOTAL DEPOSITS	
EXPENSES		EXPENSES		EXPENSES	
DATE SPENT		DATE SPENT		DATE SPENT	
FOR:		FOR:		FOR:	
DATE SPENT		DATE SPENT		DATE SPENT	
FOR:		FOR:		FOR:	
TOTAL SPENT		TOTAL SPENT		TOTAL SPENT	
ENDING BALANCE		ENDING BALANCE		ENDING BALANCE	

GOALS MONITORING FORM NO. 3

Record dates and entries for a reading compared to Goals.

HOUSEHOLD ACCOUNT

CATEGORY GROCERIES	GOAL	CATEGORY MEALS OUT	GOAL	CATEGORY	GOAL
DATE SPENT		DATE SPENT		DATE SPENT	
DATE SPENT		DATE SPENT		DATE SPENT	
TOTAL TO DATE		TOTAL TO DATE		TOTAL TO DATE	
DATE SPENT		DATE SPENT		DATE SPENT	
TOTAL TO DATE		TOTAL TO DATE		TOTAL TO DATE	
DATE SPENT		DATE SPENT		DATE SPENT	
TOTAL TO DATE		TOTAL TO DATE		TOTAL TO DATE	
DATE SPENT		DATE SPENT		DATE SPENT	
TOTAL TO DATE		TOTAL TO DATE		TOTAL TO DATE	
DATE SPENT		DATE SPENT		DATE SPENT	
TOTAL TO DATE		TOTAL TO DATE		TOTAL TO DATE	
DATE SPENT		DATE SPENT		DATE SPENT	
TOTAL TO DATE		TOTAL TO DATE		TOTAL TO DATE	

GOALS MONITORING FORM NO. 4

Record dates and entries for a reading compared to Goals.

GENERAL ACCOUNT

CATEGORY	GOAL	CATEGORY	GOAL	CATEGORY	GOAL
DATE SPENT		DATE SPENT		DATE SPENT	
DATE SPENT		DATE SPENT		DATE SPENT	
TOTAL TO DATE		TOTAL TO DATE		TOTAL TO DATE	
DATE SPENT		DATE SPENT		DATE SPENT	
TOTAL TO DATE		TOTAL TO DATE		TOTAL TO DATE	
DATE SPENT		DATE SPENT		DATE SPENT	
TOTAL TO DATE		TOTAL TO DATE		TOTAL TO DATE	
CATEGORY	GOAL	CATEGORY	GOAL	CATEGORY	GOAL
DATE SPENT		DATE SPENT		DATE SPENT	
DATE SPENT		DATE SPENT		DATE SPENT	
TOTAL TO DATE		TOTAL TO DATE		TOTAL TO DATE	
DATE SPENT		DATE SPENT		DATE SPENT	
TOTAL TO DATE		TOTAL TO DATE		TOTAL TO DATE	

THE NO. 5 HOUSEHOLD AND NO. 6 GENERAL ACCOUNTS

You may need to use additional monitoring in the categories where you are having difficulty in keeping your expenditures within the goal you established for each category.

Some of the categories of expenses involve only one or two expenditures a month. Examples would be a rent or mortgage payment, a monthly payment on an insurance premium, etc.

If this type of payment is easy for you to keep in mind, you do not need to make any record of such payments.

The categories of expenses that may require more detailed monitoring are the categories where there are multiple expenditures in a month, such as the Groceries and Meals Out categories in the No. 5 Household Account.

The good news is that the need for this monitoring will decrease as you get your Money Management System under control. There will come a time when the Goals Monitoring Procedure is no longer necessary and the bank account monitoring will be sufficient.

The Goals Monitoring Forms are presented on four pages, but it is probable you will only need to use a small percent of the spaces available.

The Goals Monitoring Procedure requires making and maintaining a list of all expendi-

248

tures in any category where you are having dif-
ficulty keeping your expenses within the goal
for the category.

There may be categories where you have
few expenditures in the month but still have
trouble staying within your goals. Clothing and
Entertainment might be examples. Without a rigid
procedure you might be tempted to overspend.

We suggest you go through the list of categories in the No. 5 Household and No. 6 General
Accounts and identify the categories where you
think you might overspend. Then estimate how
many monthly expenditures you think you might
have in each of those categories.

On Form No. 3 there are 12 spaces for each of
the Groceries and Meals Out categories and one
unidentified space for 12 entries to be made.

On Form No. 4 there are three spaces available for four entries and three spaces available
for six entries. If you need additional spaces for
monitoring other categories, we suggest getting
additional copies of Forms No. 3 and No. 4. The
spaces presently reserved for *Groceries* and
Meals Out can also be used for other categories.
Have additional copies made to give you plenty
of monitoring spaces.

Identify and reserve a space on Form No. 3 or
No. 4 that will give you *ample* spaces to list all
disbursements you will be making in a month in
those categories.

At the top of the reserved space, identify the category, such as Groceries, and enter the monthly goal you have established for that category.

Starting at the beginning of the month, record your expenditures by date and amount and calculate your Total To Date. You can easily compare the current Total To Date at any time of the month to your total monthly goal.

For example, your goal for Groceries might be $400 for the month. If, as of mid-month, you have spent $250, that might alert you to the need to limit your grocery purchases during the balance of the month.

MONITORING THE NO. 1 FAMILY SECURITY ACCOUNT AND THE NOS. 2, 3 AND 4 ACCRUAL ACCOUNTS

The monitoring of your No. 1 Family Security Account and Nos. 2, 3 and 4 Accrual Accounts can be very brief or more extensive, depending on how much you use the accounts.

The No. 1 Family Security Account may only involve your verifying that your planned monthly deposit was made. If there is *more* activity, such as making an investment from the account or withdrawing funds from it, you may need to make the appropriate entries in the spaces for that account in the upper space of Form No. 1.

The Family Security Account is basically a savings account. The most important point is that the planned deposit or deposits are made each month.

The best thing you can do with this account is to be sure you make your deposits each month and let your money "grow." The worst thing you can do with this account is to make frequent withdrawals.

The establishment and monitoring of accrual accounts may be a new subject to you. For that reason, there will be repetitions of the suggested procedures. We hope the repetition will be helpful to you.

A routine is recommended in monitoring each of the accrual accounts monthly. It was previously suggested that when you completed the forms for your Nos. 2, 3 and 4 Accounts you enter the *subject* of the accrual, the amount needed at spending time and the amount you need to set aside each month to be ready for the expenditures.

To prepare for later monitoring, it was suggested you calculate the amount you will need to have in your bank account to cover the needs of the next three months, six months and the year.

The balance in the bank account for each accrual account is designed to ensure you have necessary funds ready for the disbursements.

To the *end-of-the-month balance* in your bank account, *add* the planned monthly deposits, *minus* planned expenditures, to make sure you will have the needed funds in the next three months, six months, and the year points.

A glance at the balance of the bank account may be sufficient. You may need to make some calculations to project the status of the bank account at the future monthly points.

It is suggested the Nos. 2, 3 and 4 Accrual Accounts be on a calendar-year basis.

The No. 2 Main Accrual Account was primarily designed to fit annual needs such as real estate taxes not included in a monthly mortgage payment, annual or semi-annual insurance premiums, annual automobile taxes and license registrations, etc.

It is suggested that short-term subjects like a note coming due in three months might be handled and *monitored* separately rather than through the Main Accrual Account.

The timing of the month in which you establish your accrual accounts will be important. In the Christmas and Gift Account your greatest expenditures will occur in December. In the Vacation Account the greatest expenditure will be made in the month you decide to take your major vacation.

A simultaneous starting of all accrual accounts is highly desirable. If a complete plan is not established, there is always a temptation for unplanned funds to get lost and be spent on unplanned desires.

The ideal time to start your Christmas and Gift Account is 12 months before December. The ideal time to start your Vacation Account is 12 months before your major vacation.

As you developed your information on the Master Forms Nos. 2, 3 and 4, you indicated the amount you wanted to have available in the various months of the year. That total divided by 12 gave you the amount you needed to set aside each month to provide the funds.

At the bottom of each of those Master Forms you calculated the amount you would need to have on hand to meet your planned expenditures in the next three months, six months and the year.

To monitor these accounts each month you need to compare the balance in your bank account to your needs on your accrual account form. The purpose is to make sure you are on target with the amount you are planning on spending in each account each month.

Will you have sufficient funds on hand in three months? At the going rate of the deposit each month, will you have sufficient funds on hand in six months? And in the year? Think of it as an arithmetic problem.

As you start these accounts, you may have temporary shortages because you haven't had time to build up sufficient funds. If that situation develops, you will need to increase your monthly deposit or cut your spending to come out even.

253

In time, your deposit will equal your planned spending, so don't give up on the plan.

If your amount of money available is limited, you might, as you start the account, have to limit the amount you want to spend in order to give you more time to set aside the money. You may want to get a bookkeeper, accountant or someone good with figures to help you make the computations as you get started. The final results will be worth the effort.

The Main Accrual Account will take a bit more planning. We suggest your expenditures from this account also be on a 12-month, calendar-year basis. These expenditures would include real estate taxes due at the end of the year if they have not already been set aside as part of a mortgage payment, annual insurance premiums due at various times of the year, automobile taxes and license renewals, quarterly income tax payments or estimates due, etc.

Other expenditures may develop through the year that you want to pay through this account.

On Forms Nos. 2, 3 and 4, there will be a line to enter your planning of the amount of the deposit needed in the various months of the year.

In the Main Accrual Account, *new* needs and entries may develop throughout the year that you want to pay through this account. We have suggested these subjects be monitored separately, but the money can be set aside in the appropriate bank account.

254

On Master Form No. 2, you will need to plan the amount that will be needed at a certain time and then calculate the number of months you have to get ready.

Before you commit to a plan for a future expenditure, you will need to be sure you can set aside a sufficient amount each month to be ready for the expenditure when it becomes due.

On the accrual accounts, we strongly suggest you set aside and deposit the same amounts each month rather than changing from month to month. That will produce a larger balance on hand in some months than in others. With this balance, you will be confident you will have adequate funds in the months with the highest expenditures. If you plan expenditures early in the year, you will need to start accruing those funds the necessary months in advance.

ALTERNATIVE APPROACH

On the premise your income and availability of funds will remain at one level, we suggest the Main Accrual Account be established on the basis you will have a specific total annual amount to be placed and spent from that account.

You can plan on setting aside money for real estate taxes, planned expenditures, debt reductions, etc., but there will be no money available for other items until some obligations are paid or your income and monthly deposits increase.

The three accrual accounts need to be established on the basis you have only so much money available each month to fund the accounts. This will require you to establish your spending limits through the three accrual accounts *in total* and then with an amount for each of the accounts.

THE ENVELOPE SYSTEM

Some households may need to consider using the "Envelope System." We did not invent it, but it is good for families who must spend *each dollar* very, very carefully.

If Form Nos. 1, 2, 3 and 4 on the Goals Monitoring Form do not give you positive control, you may need to use the Envelope System.

Under the Envelope System, cash is placed in several envelopes at the beginning of a week or two-week spending period. The envelope should be identified with the category name and spent for only the *specified* use. The important point is to control the cash and prevent any of it from being spent for other purposes.

In both the Household and General Accounts, there are categories generally paid with cash. This would involve parking fees, lunches, toiletries, etc.

On the Master Form No. 5, Household Account, we have listed the category "petty cash." On the Master Form No. 6, General Account, we have listed "petty cash." Cash placed in envelopes for each of these categories will be done by the person responsible for each of the accounts.

Heads of households might each estimate the amount of cash they will need for an *average day* and put that amount, times the number of days, like in a week, in envelopes.

These might be called the heads of household "petty cash" accounts. They then can check their envelopes every day or two to make sure they are staying within their individual spending limits.

Cash for two or three small expense categories might be consolidated into one "Miscellaneous" envelope.

Children's weekly allowances also could be put in envelopes. That would be a great learning experience for them!

An important possible use of the Envelope System would be placing cash in an envelope to cover all of your Groceries expenses for the coming week. Then be careful some of that money doesn't get spent for other things.

Without the bank account system, you will need to use *more envelopes* to cover all of the categories of expenses. If you *are using bank accounts* or the *Goals Monitoring Procedure*, you will *need fewer or no envelopes*.

If you use the Envelope System, you will have to protect the envelopes and make sure one envelope's cash is not being spent to cover the needs of another envelope.

Whichever follow-through method you choose to use: bank accounts, posting the Goals Monitoring Forms by hand, using the Envelope System or a combination of all of those procedures, you will achieve your money management success only if you are *determined* to do so.

PART VI
SPECIAL SUBJECTS OF INTEREST
TO SOME READERS —

259

A METHOD OF REDUCING DEBTS AND AVOIDING BANKRUPTCY

Many families face the situation of having more debts and payments coming due than they have money to make the payments.

One solution is to get all of your creditors (people to whom you owe money) to agree on a plan which will give you *more time* to pay off your debts. The project may not be easy, but it is not impossible.

There is no general plan that will fit all situations. Your objective should be to keep your plan as easy to understand as possible.

The first step is to determine the amount you have available each month, after living expenses, for debt reduction. The next step will be to develop a complete list of your creditors, the amount you owe each of them and pertinent information concerning each of the debts.

There are three steps in developing the information on the amount you will have available each month for debt reduction. The first step will be to develop solid information on what your income will be in an average month.

If your income varies from month to month, it would be advisable to use figures from your lowest income months. Next, make a list of your living expenses in a month. Subtracting the amount of your living expenses from your income will tell you the amount of money you have available for debt reduction.

That will be a very important figure in developing your plan on how you are going to work your way out of debt.

When the time comes for you to present your plan to your creditors, you may need to assure them the payments on your home and car are in line with your income and do not adversely affect your ability to make payments on other debts.

We suggest you estimate your living expenses slightly on the high side. You then will be confident the remaining amount of your income will be ample to make the planned payments. This will be important in case you encounter some unexpected expenses which could leave you short of promised dollars for your creditors.

The worst mistake you might make is to think you will have more money available for debt payments each month than you will actually have.

If you underestimate your monthly living expenses, you will be short of the amount you will need for promised debt payments. Then you will find yourselves in the position where you cannot make all of the agreed payments and have to start your plan all over.

If you overestimate your monthly living expenses, you will have more money available and can make larger payments than you agreed to make. That will also give you a safety margin if unexpected living expenses develop. The important point is that you want to be certain you can fulfill all promises made to your creditors.

You will need to make a list of all of your debts. This should include the name of the creditor, the date the debt was incurred, the original amount due, the present amount due, if it is a secured or unsecured obligation, the monthly payment and the number of months to pay. Any interest or charges involved should be computed and included in the monthly payment. There will be a form at the end of this chapter to assist you in developing the list. This form will fit most situations. If not, you may need to develop your own form.

After you have developed the above figures on income available for debt reduction and your total debts, the challenge will be how you will divide the amount available. Your big challenge will be to work out the plan you think is best for all creditors and hope they will agree with it.

You probably will have different types of creditors that will make it difficult in developing a plan which they feel is fair to all of them.

An important point is that payments on home or car mortgages probably will need to be given priority because, if they are not paid, you will risk losing your home or car.

A common mistake is to yield to the temptation to totally pay off small obligations rather than writing more checks each month over a period of time. There is also a temptation to favor creditors whom you feel have accorded you special consideration. That would make it very difficult for some of your creditors to understand why others are being favored. Try to treat all creditors equally with no favoritism to any of them.

There will be other differences among your creditors that may need to be considered. You may have to favor creditors who are not charging you interest or lower interest than other creditors. Another creditor may have made you a loan at a very critical time, and you feel you should take that into consideration.

There probably will be other factors you feel you should consider in developing your plan. It will be important you be prepared to explain and justify why it may seem you are favoring some creditors over others.

After you have developed your plan, you will need to be prepared to present it to each of them. It probably would be preferable to present to each creditor the plan relating to them only. If they are satisfied with the plan for them, you do not have to give them details about other creditors. It may be necessary to give your creditors your complete plan involving all creditors.

Most of your creditors will go along with the plan you present to them if they feel they are being treated fairly and if they are confident you will make the payments you promise to make.

The threat of bankruptcy has lost its effectiveness with many creditors. The best approach with many creditors in this era is to assure them you are doing the very best that you can, but if your plan is not acceptable, the creditors and you will have to face difficult consequences. You might state that you do not even want to consider bankruptcy and are trying to establish a plan that will be good for everyone involved.

Some of your creditors will be patient and understanding, and some will not be. Don't yield to the pressure of one or two of your unsecured creditors and favor them with larger payments. If any of your creditors are too uncooperative, you will have to fall back on the fact that if you do not get cooperation you will have to resort to bankruptcy. That statement of fact will generally increase their spirit of cooperation.

If your creditors go along with your plan, it will be extremely important you keep your word in making all payments in the amounts promised and on time. If, for any reason, you cannot keep those promises, it will be very important you advise all of your creditors promptly and advise them of the facts. Favoring one creditor over another probably will get you into deeper trouble than anything else.

You should be prepared to explain to your creditors you have an assortment of creditors with varying situations and you are trying to be fair to all concerned. The main concern of each of your creditors is probably going to be that you give them confidence you will make your promised payments on time with the ultimate goal that all will be paid in full.

There are many people who feel that if they could merge all of their debts and make just one payment per month, their problems would be over. A few words on that subject might be helpful.

To merge all of your debts, you would need to get a bank or someone to loan you enough money to pay off all of your obligations. That probably would be very difficult but perhaps not impossible.

You would then, however, have to pay interest on that obligation. If your creditors were not charging you interest, there would be a cost to you for consolidating your debts. The cost of writing one check per month to one creditor instead of several checks to creditors might possibly be too high a price to pay for the convenience.

There may come a time when you feel your financial problems are too big for you to handle by yourselves. If so, we recommend you get in touch with Consumer Credit Counseling Services Inc. They are a not-for-profit organization with offices in all states, many cities in the United States and also around the world.

They can assist you in analyzing your problems and preparing the information for your creditors. They also may negotiate with your creditors to develop a solution. In some circumstances, they may charge a modest fee and other circumstances donate their services.

In the United States, you can phone (800) 388-2227 to get the location of their nearest office.

Creditor	Date of Debt	Original Amount	Present Amount	Secured		Monthly Payment	Number Of Months To Pay
				Yes	No		

INCREASING YOUR INCOME AS A WAY TO HELP MEET YOUR GOALS

There may come a time when you feel you have cut all of your expenses as much as you can and still don't have enough money to provide all of the things you need or desire. If you reach that point, the next challenge is to give more attention to increasing your income.

ACQUIRING ADDITIONAL SKILLS

The laws of supply and demand generally determine the price at which products sell. Products with a higher quality generally sell for a higher price.

The same general principles apply to the compensation people are paid. The higher the qualifications, the higher the compensation. This system provides encouragement to develop more skills, perhaps through a special vocational or college class, or a home study course.

In most industries there are opportunities to demonstrate over a period of time that you have abilities that justify your moving up the compensation ladder. That might result from doing the same type of work but doing it better than your fellow employees. It also might mean you are demonstrating greater degrees of dependability and responsibility.

Increasing your income as a means of meeting your financial goals might involve developing new and different skills with your present employer that merit more compensation. It might be a new skill that your present employer cannot use but would make you more valuable to another employer.

This might encourage continuing your education toward general or specific goals.

Developing or increasing computer skills are very important stepping stones for many people. Home computers are a good place to start in that field.

Don't overlook the possibility of increasing your skills and compensation as an aid in mastering your money management challenges.

A SECOND SOURCE OF INCOME

Many people increase their income by working extra part-time jobs. There *are* only so many hours in a day for family, friends and yourself. Fortunately there are ways to supplement your regular income without sacrificing all of those important priorities in life.

Do you have a hobby or a skill that others can use? Many individuals are looking for someone to do odd jobs, especially after normal working hours. Their needs might include home repairs, lawn work, sewing, typing papers for students, other computer work, driving a car for senior citizens, getting paid for sports officiating or weekend work at a marina, service station or restaurant, just to name a few.

You can go door-to-door in residential neighborhoods seeking jobs. Posting a notice on a senior center or community bulletin board advertising your skills and availability is likely to bring you extra work. Make your information easily readable.

Advertising in the want ads is another way to find jobs. Once you get your first few customers, others will hear about you through word of mouth. An initial investment in a classified ad could pay big dividends.

Seasonal work or work you can do at home is always a possibility. Check the classifieds for opportunities for part-time work. There are countless possibilities, and extra dollars per week could make your money management easier!

PLANNING FOR MONEY THAT WILL BE NEEDED IN FUTURE YEARS

Most of the chapters in this book relate to what might be called "routine" problems that individuals and families face in money management. Some subjects that had previously been considered routine or secondary now are requiring *additional* planning.

Those subjects include the increasing costs of college educations for children and a couple's needs for more money than they had previously planned for their retirement years.

FUNDS FOR COLLEGE EDUCATIONS

The cost of a college education is increasing faster than the rate of inflation. The expenses for tuition, fees, room and board at both public and private institutions have nearly doubled over the past ten years. The rate of inflation is predicted to continue. If so, the cost of a college education can be expected to follow the same pattern.

The primary college education costs (tuition, fees and room and board) at four-year institutions now range from $5,000, in *less than a dozen colleges*, to a high of almost $34,000 per year.

The average increase in tuition and fees from the previous year for all colleges has now reached 4.4 percent. Using a 4 percent increasing rate, the cost 20 years from now will range from approximately $10,000 for the few schools now costing $5,000, to $69,000 *per year* for the school now costing $34,000.

The 4 percent figure is for a relatively short time. For a long-range estimate, inflation projections must be recognized. Leaders in the education field estimate the cost of a college education will increase at approximately twice the current overall inflation rate of 3 percent.

For purposes of an analysis of this impact on your money management system, assume that you will invest funds monthly at a return of 6 percent, which appears to represent the annual increase in college costs.

To keep the following projection as simple as possible, we will assume that the projected cost of the four-year education will be saved by the *beginning* of the first year of college. This will provide some extra funds at the beginning of college days.

The following chart will confirm the future impact on your monthly money management system and your need to plan.

FUNDING COLLEGE WITH MONTHLY INVESTMENTS EARNING SIX PERCENT

Estimated 4 year cost	$40,000		
Number of years to save	5	10	15
Monthly savings necessary	$773	$444	$337

Estimated 4 year cost	$60,000		
Number of years to save	5	10	15
Monthly savings necessary	$1,160	$666	$506

Estimated 4 year cost	$80,000		
Number of years to save	5	10	15
Monthly savings necessary	$1,547	$888	$675

Those figures pose big problems on how to face the challenge of accumulating that much money. Another problem to face is that students in college 20 years from now probably will have greater difficulty in being able to work their way through.

New York Life Insurance Co. prints a booklet titled, "College Costs, (Each Year) Edition." There is information if you are interested in costs for a specific college. This booklet is updated annually and is available through local representatives of the company or by mail at 51 Madison Avenue, New York, NY 10010 or www.newyorklife.com on the Internet.

SECTION 529 COLLEGE SAVINGS PLANS

In the past 20 years, as previously indicated, the cost of a college education has increased faster than the rate of inflation. With that trend the cost of many college degrees in 20 years may approach $118,000 at a public school and up to $260,000 at a private school. These costs do not include graduate school.

This can be overwhelming to students and their families. Financial aid or scholarships will not be sufficient for every student's needs. Students may not be able to "work their way" through college. The burden of student loans may start students off at a financial disadvantage after they graduate.

Many families want to make sure a college education is an option available for their children. The level of savings needed can be intimidating. For many families, the cost of college educations for their children is the largest expense they will ever have.

Fortunately, help is available through *Section 529 plans* currently available in 41 states, as authorized by Congress in 1996. These plans will help some parents achieve their college savings goals.

Section 529 plans have many benefits. Each state's plan is somewhat different. In general, money placed in a college savings plan grows tax-free until the money is withdrawn to pay qualified education expenses.

The plans are administered by the state or a state-selected investment company. Most plans provide a mix of stocks and bonds. The investment mix often is based on the age of the child and your risk tolerance. Anyone can make a contribution to the account, including grandparents and family friends.

When college days are reached, distributions are completely tax free if used for qualified educational expenses. The earnings portion of those not used for qualified educational expenses is taxed at the student's tax rate, which is likely lower than the donor's.

The money can be used at any accredited postsecondary school in the United States. This includes state universities, public community colleges, private colleges, technical schools and vocational schools.

Qualified expenses can be for tuition, room and board, books, etc. These savings plans detract little or nothing from the child's potential scholarship financial aid awards.

If a grandparent wants to make a gift to reduce the size of his or her estate for gift tax purposes, he or she can contribute a lump sum of $50,000 per beneficiary without gift tax concerns, provided they make no other gifts to those beneficiaries in the same year or next four years. States have various limitations and guidelines, but the following gives the general picture.

Generally the contribution and its earnings are no longer part of the parent's, grandparent's or other's taxable estate. However, until the money is withdrawn, it remains in the control of the plan's trustee.

In most circumstances it is possible to change beneficiaries from one family member to another or even withdraw the money for the donor's use. A penalty is applied if a withdrawal is made for use other than educational expenses. There are other allowable exceptions such as the beneficiary's death or disability, or the beneficiary's reception of a scholarship.

Earnings on investments in the plan are exempt from federal and state income taxes unless withdrawn for non-education purposes.

Residents of one state can utilize the plan of another state subject to some restrictions. In fact, some states have created a tax deduction or credit for contributions to these plans. (For example, in Kansas up to $2,000 per donor, per student, per year can be deducted from Kansas taxable income.)

The important thing is not where or how you start saving for college expenses but rather that you begin planning and saving early. There are several charts in this book demonstrating how money "grows" over a period of years. Be sure to keep this in mind as you consider college savings plans with their tax benefits.

There is much information on the Internet on this subject.

EDUCATION RELATED INCOME TAX CREDITS AVAILABLE

In addition to college savings plans, there are two education related income tax credits available when expenses are paid: the Hope scholarship credit and the lifetime learning credit.

These credits may be claimed on tax returns by individuals for tuition expenses incurred by students pursuing college or graduate degrees or vocational training.

The Hope scholarship credit allows a maximum credit of $1,500 per student for each of the first two years of post-secondary education.

The lifetime learning credit is calculated as 20 percent of qualified tuition expenses paid by the taxpayer for any year the Hope credit is not claimed.

Each credit is available only for certain qualifying expenses, and the credits are reduced between specified income phaseout ranges.

In addition, after 2001, coordination rules are available so that a taxpayer may claim credits and take distributions from a college savings plan in the same year. They just need to be for different dollars spent on qualified expenses.

Two deductions are also available related to education expenses: the student loan interest deduction and a higher education deduction.

If any of these credits or deductions are of interest to you, you should contact your tax advisor or financial planner.

BUILDING INCOME NEEDED IN RETIREMENT YEARS

Another big problem faces many couples. It is that Social Security will not be adequate to support a couple at the income level they will desire in their retirement years.

The need to start planning as early as possible for income needed in retirement years has become more important than ever. Those facing retirement in the extended future are faced with an increasing need for financial planning.

For those facing these challenges, it may be helpful to have a simple guide in calculating how much money you need to set aside to supplement your retirement income.

In order to accomplish these calculations, you need to develop the answers to the following three questions.

1. How much annual income over and above Social Security and other retirement income will you need?
2. How many years until you retire?
3. How many years will you probably live after retirement?

There will be information following that will help you estimate the answers to the questions. With the answers, you can use the following tables to assist you in planning your needs in your retirement years.

280

CALCULATION OF
SUPPLEMENTAL INCOME NEEDED

How much annual income do
you estimate you will need in
today's dollars after you
retire?

Less: Estimated annual Social
Security benefits.

Less: Annual distributions
from employer benefits,
401(K) plans, investments, etc.

Net: Additional supplemental
income you will need.

ESTIMATING NUMBER OF YEARS YOU WILL LIVE AFTER RETIREMENT

LIFE EXPECTANCY TABLE USED BY LIFE INSURANCE COMPANIES

At This Age	Years of Life Expectancy Remaining		At This Age	Years of Life Expectancy Remaining	
	Male	Female		Male	Female
30	43	48	50	25	30
31	42	47	51	25	29
32	41	46	52	24	28
33	40	45	53	23	27
34	40	44	54	22	26
35	39	43	55	21	25
36	38	42	56	21	24
37	37	41	57	20	24
38	36	40	58	19	23
39	35	39	59	18	22
40	34	38	60	18	21
41	33	37	61	17	20
42	32	37	62	16	20
43	31	36	63	15	19
44	31	35	64	15	18
45	30	34	65	14	17
46	29	33	66	13	17
47	28	32	67	13	16
48	27	31	68	12	15
49	26	30	69	12	14

SUPPLEMENTAL RETIREMENT INCOME ADJUSTED FOR INFLATION AND INVESTMENTS.

We are now ready to calculate how much additional funds you need to set aside to provide for your supplemental retirement income. Tables A, B and C are on the next pages.

From Exhibit 1 – The amount of annual supplemental income that you will need.

(1) ☐

From Table A – The rate based on your anticipated rate of return and estimated years after retirement

(2) ☐

Multiply (1) by (2) – This is the present value upon retirement of the amount needed to fund the annual income desired. This calculation assumes that all funds will be exhausted upon death.

(3) ☐

From Table B – The rate based on your estimate of the inflation rate and estimated years until retirement.

(4) ☐

(Continued on Next Page)

**Multiply (3) by (4) – This provides
you with an inflation adjusted
amount that you will need to
fund the annual income needed.   (5)**

**From Table C – The annual growth
factor by estimating your assumed
interest rate and estimated years
until retirement.   (6)**

**Divide (5) by (6) – This provides you
with an annual amount that you
will need to invest each year to
reach your goal.   (7)**

TABLE A – GROWTH AFTER RETIREMENT

		Life expectancy after retirement				
		10 yrs	15 yrs	20 yrs	25 yrs	30 yrs
Rate of	5%	7.678	10.299	12.340	13.931	15.171
Return	6%	7.302	9.607	11.315	12.582	13.521
	7%	6.949	8.978	10.408	11.417	12.129
	8%	6.620	8.405	9.603	10.407	10.946
	9%	6.311	7.883	8.886	9.527	9.936

TABLE B – INFLATION FACTORS

		Number of years until retirement						
		5 yrs	10 yrs	15 yrs	20 yrs	25 yrs	30 yrs	35 yrs
Inflation	3%	1.159	1.344	1.558	1.806	2.094	2.427	2.814
Rate	4%	1.217	1.480	1.801	2.191	2.666	3.243	3.946
	5%	1.276	1.628	2.078	2.653	3.386	4.321	5.516
	6%	1.338	1.791	2.397	3.207	4.292	5.743	7.686
	7%	1.403	1.967	2.759	3.870	5.427	7.612	10.677
	8%	1.469	2.158	3.172	4.660	6.848	10.062	14.785
	9%	1.538	2.367	3.642	5.604	8.623	13.267	20.414

TABLE C – INVESTMENT GROWTH

		Number of years until retirement						
		5 yrs	10 yrs	15 yrs	20 yrs	25 yrs	30 yrs	35 yrs
Rate of	5%	5.525	12.578	21.579	33.066	47.727	66.439	90.320
Return	6%	5.637	13.181	23.276	36.786	54.865	79.058	111.435
	7%	5.751	13.816	25.129	40.995	63.249	94.461	138.237
	8%	5.866	14.486	27.152	45.761	73.105	113.283	172.317
	9%	5.985	15.193	29.361	51.160	84.701	136.308	215.711

The following is an example of the previous Supplemental Retirement Calculation:

A 35-year-old individual wants to start planning for retirement. In addition to his anticipated social security and pension plan, he would like to have an additional $20,000 per year (in today's dollars) in supplemental retirement income. He estimates the annual inflation rate to be 3 percent and believes he will retire at age 65. He believes he will live to be 80 years old and that 6 percent is a reasonable rate of return on investments.

From Exhibit 1 – The amount of annual supplemental income that you will need   (1) $20,000

From Table A – The rate based on your anticipated rate of return and estimated years after retirement   (2)   9.607

Multiply (1) by (2) – This is the present value upon retirement of the amount needed to fund the annual income desired. This calculation assumes that all funds will be exhausted upon death.   (3) $192,140

(Continued on Next Page)

**From Table B – The rate based
on your estimate of the
inflation rate and estimated
years until retirement.** (4) | 2.427 |

**Multiply (3) by (4) – This provides
you with an inflation adjusted
amount that you will need to
fund the annual income needed.** (5) | $466,323 |

**From Table C – The annual growth
factor by estimating your assumed
interest rate and estimated years
until retirement.** (6) | 79.058 |

**Divide (5) by (6) – This provides
you with an annual amount that
you will need to invest each year
to reach your goal.** (7) | $5,898 |

The amount of income an individual or a couple will need upon retirement, minus the income of which they are confident, will demonstrate the need for their additional planning to meet their needs.

SETTING MONEY ASIDE FOR OTHER SPECIAL NEEDS

How many times have you said, "We wish we would have set aside money to take care of this?"

The following charts demonstrate how you can invest funds over a period of time in order to accumulate a desired amount.

These charts are based on a 3 percent per year inflation factor and assuming a 6 percent rate of return on your investments.

EXAMPLE:

If an individual knows that he will need $25,000 for a down payment on a house that he plans on purchasing in 5 years, he can calculate his monthly amount that needs to be set aside as follows:

1. What is the total amount desired at the end of the term? $25,000

2. Inflation factor from table below based on number of years.   <u>1.159</u>

3. Multiply Line 1 by Line 2 – This is your desired amount in future dollars. $28,975

4. Investment factor from table below based on number of years.   <u>0.010573</u>

5. Multiply Line 3 by Line 4 – This is your required monthly savings.   <u>$306.35</u>

288

CALCULATE YOUR OWN MONTHLY INVESTMENTS NEEDED

Using the formula below, you can calculate your own required monthly investments. All you need to know is how many years you will be investing for and how much in "today's" dollars you want to have at the end of this time.

1. What is the total amount desired
   at the end of the term? $_____

2. Inflation factor from table below
   based on number of years.   _____

3. Multiply Line 1 by Line 2 – This
   is your desired amount in future
   dollars.   _____

4. Investment factor from table below
   based on number of years.   _____

5. Multiply Line 3 by Line 4 – This
   Is your required monthly
   investment. $_____

RATIOS:

	INFLATION FACTORS	INVESTMENT FACTORS
1 YEAR	1.030	0.0759767
2 YEARS	1.060	0.0391245
5 YEARS	1.159	0.0105729
10 YEARS	1.344	0.0060714
15 YEARS	1.558	0.0034217
20 YEARS	1.806	0.0021534
25 YEARS	2.094	0.0014360
30 YEARS	2.427	0.0009905
35 YEARS	2.814	0.0006983

SELECTED EXAMPLES:

DESIRED AMOUNT AT THE END OF YEARS IN TODAY'S DOLLARS

NUMBER OF YEARS TO INVEST	$1,000	$5,000	$10,000	$15,000
	REQUIRED MONTHLY SAVINGS AND INVESTMENT			
1 YEAR	$78.26	$391.28	$782.56	$1,173.84
2 YEARS	$41.47	$207.36	$414.72	$622.08
5 YEARS	$12.25	$61.27	$122.54	$183.81
10 YEARS	$8.16	$40.80	$81.60	$122.40
15 YEARS	$5.33	$26.66	$53.31	$79.97
20 YEARS	$3.89	$19.45	$38.89	$58.34
25 YEARS	$3.01	$15.04	$30.07	$45.11
30 YEARS	$2.40	$12.02	$24.04	$36.06
35 YEARS	$1.97	$9.83	$19.65	$29.48

DESIRED AMOUNT AT THE END OF YEARS IN TODAYS DOLLARS

	$20,000	$25,000	$50,000	$100,000
NUMBER OF YEARS TO INVEST	**REQUIRED MONTHLY SAVINGS AND INVESTMENT**			

	$20,000	$25,000	$50,000	$100,000
1 YEAR	$1,565.12	$1,956.40	$3,912.80	$7,825.60
2 YEARS	$829.44	$1,036.80	$2,073.60	$4,147.20
5 YEARS	$245.08	$306.35	$612.70	$1,225.40
10 YEARS	$163.20	$204.00	$408.00	$816.00
15 YEARS	$106.62	$133.28	$266.55	$533.10
20 YEARS	$77.78	$97.23	$194.45	$388.90
25 YEARS	$60.14	$75.18	$150.35	$300.70
30 YEARS	$48.08	$60.10	$120.20	$240.40
35 YEARS	$39.30	$49.13	$98.25	$196.50

NEW OPPORTUNITIES FOR RETIREMENT INVESTING

In 2002, you will be able to make larger contributions to your Individual Retirement Account due to the tax relief act passed in the spring of 2001. The contribution limit for IRAs will increase to $3,000 from $2,000 in 2002. Annual limits will continue to rise, reaching $4,000 in 2005 and $5,000 in 2008.

If you are 50 or older, the new law also allows you to "catch up" on your retirement savings by making additional contributions. For Roth and Traditional IRAs, the additional contribution allowance is $500 from 2002 to 2005 and $1,000 in 2006 and thereafter. That means those who are 50 and older can contribute $3,500 annually from 2002 to 2004; $4,500 in 2005; $5,000 in 2006 and 2007; and $6,000 in 2008.

As with any decisions, you should consult with your tax advisor before making any decisions related to tax planning.

A REVERSE MORTGAGE
AS A SOURCE OF FUNDS

A couple in their retirement years might find that, despite their best efforts, they are in need of funds. A "reverse mortgage" might be a possibility.

An essential factor is that they have a substantial equity in their home. The plan might be described as a home equity loan with a special purpose, receiving a specified amount of money each month for several years.

One plan might be for the property owners to get a first or second mortgage on their home. If they receive the funds in one lump disbursement, it can then be used to invest in an annuity from an insurance company that will pay them a specified amount for a stated period of time.

The balance due on the mortgage given to secure the annuity must then be paid through the sale of the property on a stated date or upon the deaths of the property owners.

The monthly disbursement to the property owners might also be made directly by the bank or other lending institution instead of through the purchase of an annuity. There would be a stated limit on the disbursement to them and the total obligation would probably have to be satisfied by the sale of the home. The bank would plan for there to be some equity in the property at the final due date in order to protect them against loss. In that event the property owners would receive the margin of the equity.

Senior property owners in need of money might benefit from discussing this plan with their bank or other lending institution.

PART VII
THE GRAND FINALE

HOW YOU CAN SAVE HERE AND THERE AND BECOME A MILLIONAIRE

The first two chapters in this book were "Opening The Doors of Opportunity" and "The Magic of Compounding — The Master Chart on How Money Grows."

Those first chapters showed how saving small dollar amounts per month and depositing or investing the savings can grow over a period of years to very large amounts.

In those chapters and reviewed in this chapter there are many examples of amounts that can be saved.

Attention was called to the difference between essential and discretionary spending. The first key to accumulating dollars lies in keeping a tight limit on what is essential.

The second key is to not let money that is saved remain idle. Idle money has a way of slipping into unplanned expenditures. Put idle money to work by immediately depositing or investing it. You need to use the "one-two punch." Number 1 — *Save* it. Number 2 — *Invest* it.

THE BASIC FORMULA

1. Think of *every* subject of expense as an *opportunity* to *save*.
2. Those savings might be on an annual basis, semiannual basis, quarterly basis or weekly basis. You will then need to convert them into monthly depositing or investing figures to achieve maximum compounding. The following charts are therefore based upon the amounts that can be saved and compounded monthly.
3. Deposit or invest that money every month where it will be compounded monthly at an annual rate of 5 percent.

Charts earlier in the book and in this chapter will demonstrate how your monthly deposits or investments will grow over a period of years.

If you accepted the challenge to "Save Some, Spend Some," you are on your way to accumulating many dollars. If you haven't started on that program, it is never too late to start, like *RIGHT NOW!*

Here are some guidelines on how to use the charts and information that will follow.

On some expenses there are specific items and figures on the amounts that can be saved and invested monthly. One example would be the savings you can achieve by not smoking a specified number of packs of cigarettes. On other subjects like groceries, there will be a total covering all groceries but with no specific examples.

Another important example will be the amount you can save by building or buying a slightly smaller house. That savings starts with your determining the amount of money you will have available each month to pay on a mortgage. The next step is to build or buy a slightly smaller house with, for example, a 20 percent lower mortgage. With the lower mortgage you will have a smaller monthly payment to make. You then can place the amount saved on the mortgage into a savings account or investment each month that will *grow* at the same time you are *reducing* the amount on your mortgage.

There are other items like automobiles, hobbies and entertainment, interest on credit card debts, groceries, clothing, and lotteries and gambling that provide opportunities to save. You will have to develop your own figures on those subjects on how much you can save and deposit monthly. There will be charts showing how small amounts saved monthly can grow into very large amounts in a number of years.

We have included examples of carpooling or the number of cans of pop per day as examples of small savings that can grow to significant amounts. The decisions are yours!

Where there are no specific examples of what savings might be achieved, we are presenting a range of small, medium and large dollar amounts of savings. You can select the amounts that fit your financial situation and your goals.

Just select the amount you feel you can save and the chart will then show you the amount to which that amount of monthly savings will grow over a period of years. The growth of those savings will provide much greater family security and happiness for everyone at all income levels.

Here are examples of the *timing of your starting* your monthly deposits or investments.

On cigarettes when you stop smoking. On credit card interest when you stop or reduce the amount of interest you have been paying. On automobiles when you move down to a less expensive car or cars. On groceries as you shop more wisely, use coupons and buy less already prepared foods. On telephone and television services, entertainment, etc. as you cut those expenses. On housing when you plan a lower mortgage and payment and provide cash you can place in a savings account or investment every month.

If you haven't been smoking but have not been saving that amount, it probably means you have been letting that amount of money slip through your hands for other expenses. To achieve the same benefits as stopping smoking, you will have to stop that slippage of the same number of dollars so you will have it available to save and invest.

HOUSING

Refer as necessary to the chapter on Housing, page 106.

Housing presents great opportunities to save and make money grow by decreasing the monthly amount of your mortgage payment and depositing or investing the savings every month.

Example A: On a 30-year $75,000 mortgage, the monthly payment at 8 $1/2$ percent interest would be $577 per month.   On a $68,500 mortgage the payment would be $527 per month, a $50 per month savings.

Example B:
$150,000 mortgage — $1,153 monthly payment
$136,950 mortgage — $1,053 monthly payment
A savings of $100 per month.

Example C:
$300,000 mortgage — $2,307 monthly payment
$274,000 mortgage — $2,107 monthly payment
A savings of $200 per month.

Example D:
$600,000 mortgage — $4,613 monthly payment
$548,000 mortgage — $4,213 monthly payment
A savings of $400 per month.

Determine the total mortgage payment you can make out of your income in a month. Buy a house with a lower monthly mortgage payment. Deposit the difference of $50 to $400 each month at 5 percent annual interest compounded monthly and watch it grow in the 30-year span of the mortgage. Then continue the savings for 10 more years and enjoy what you will save in 40 years.

Monthly savings and deposit	Will grow to these amounts in the years indicated			
	10 years	20 years	30 years	40 years
$50	$7,796	$20,638	$41,787	$76,619
$100	$15,593	$41,275	$83,574	$153,238
$200	$31,186	$82,551	$167,148	$306,476
$400	$62,372	$165,101	$334,295	$612,951

In this category in the *GRAND SUMMARY* of possible growth of money which follows, we have used a savings of $200 per month with growth to $306,476 in 40 years.

GROCERIES

Refer as necessary to the chapter on Groceries, page 123.

These savings are based on the amounts that can be achieved weekly by various size families by wise shopping, use of coupons and more home preparation followed by depositing the savings each month with a return of 5 percent per year compounded monthly.

Weekly savings	Monthly savings and deposit	Will grow to these amounts in the years indicated				
		10 years	20 years	30 years	40 years	50 years
$6	$25.00	$3,898	$10,319	$20,893	$38,309	$66,994
$12	$50.00	$7,796	$20,638	$41,786	$76,618	$133,988
$18	$75.00	$11,694	$30,957	$62,679	$114,927	$200,982
$24	$100.00	$15,592	$41,276	$83,572	$153,236	$267,976
$30	$125.00	$19,490	$51,595	$104,465	$191,545	$334,970

In this category in the *GRAND SUMMARY* of possible growth of money we have used a savings of $50 per month with growth to $76,618 in 40 years.

AUTOMOBILES

Refer as necessary to the chapter on Automobiles, page 129.

These figures are based on buying a lower priced car, saving the annual amount involved and depositing the average monthly savings each month with a return of 5 percent per year compounded monthly.

As indicated in greater detail in the chapter on Automobiles, the savings for a two car family in buying a car in the $20,000 range instead of the $25,000 range plus the savings in buying a car in the $15,000 range instead of the $20,000 range and the depositing of the savings monthly would provide $225,260 in 40 years.

Monthly savings and deposit	Will grow to these amounts in the number of years indicated compounded monthly at 5 percent per year.			
	10	20	30	40
$147	$22,922	$60,674	$122,853	$225,260

In this category in the *GRAND SUMMARY* of possible growth of money we have used a savings of $147 per month with growth to $225,260 in 40 years.

CARPOOLING

See Carpooling as mentioned in the chapter on Household Expenses and Other Hints beginning on page 138.

While this chart is presented under the name of carpooling, it is more important as a reminder of how small expenses can lead to significant amounts.

Monthly savings and deposit	Will grow to these amounts in the years indicated at 5 percent				
	10 years	20 years	30 years	40 years	50 years
$50	$7,796	$20,638	$41,787	$76,619	$133,988

In this category in the *GRAND SUMMARY* of possible growth of money we have used a savings of $50 per month with growth to $76,619 in 40 years.

POP AND OTHER BEVERAGES

Refer as necessary to the chapter on Pop and Other Beverages, page 140.

Daily Quantity —— Cost at .75	Monthly Savings and Deposit	Growth in Years Compounded Monthly at 5 Percent Per Year			
		20 years	30 years	40 years	50 years
1 can	$22.50	$9,287	$18,804	$34,479	$60,295
2 cans	$45.00	$18,574	$37,608	$68,958	$120,590
3 cans	$67.50	$27,861	$56,412	$103,437	$180,885
4 cans	$90.00	$37,148	$75,216	$137,916	$241,180

In this category in the *GRAND SUMMARY* of possible growth of money we have used a savings of $22.50 per month with growth to $34,813 in 40 years.

CIGARETTES

Refer as necessary to the chapter on Cigarettes, page 142.

The retail price of a pack of cigarettes varies based on the tax in each state.

The average price in the United States is approximately $4.25 per pack.

These savings are based on not smoking the number of packs indicated at $4.25 per pack, depositing the savings each month with a return of 5 percent per year compounded monthly.

Daily savings at $4.25 per pack	Monthly savings and deposit	Will grow to these amounts in the years indicated				
		10 years	20 years	30 years	40 years	50 years
1-$4.25	$127.50	$19,881	$52,625	$106,555	$195,378	$341,671
2-$8.50	$255.00	$39,762	$105,250	$213,110	$390,756	$683,342
3-$12.75	$382.50	$59,643	$157,875	$319,665	$586,134	$1,025,013
4-$17.00	$510.00	$79,524	$210,500	$426,220	$781,512	$1,366,684

In this category in the *GRAND SUMMARY* of possible growth of money we have used a savings of $127.50 per month with growth to $195,378 in 40 years.

HOBBIES, ENTERTAINMENT AND A BIG ETC.

Refer as necessary to the chapter on Hobbies, Entertainment and a Big Etc., page 146.

Benjamin Franklin (1706-1790) said, "Beware of little expenses. A small leak will sink a great ship." Family security is a very large ship.

Enjoy life, but be mindful that the building of family security may be more important than some pleasures of the moment.

Carefully review all of your spending under this category. Plan what you want to set aside and build for the future.

Monthly savings and deposit	Will grow to these amounts in the years indicated				
	10 years	20 years	30 years	40 years	50 years
$25	$3,898	$10,319	$20,893	$38,309	$66,994
$50	$7,796	$20,638	$41,787	$76,619	$133,989
$75	$11,695	$30,956	$62,680	$114,928	$200,983
$100	$15,593	$41,275	$83,574	$153,238	$267,977
$150	$23,389	$61,913	$125,361	$229,857	$401,965
$200	$31,186	$82,551	$167,148	$306,476	$535,954
$300	$46,779	$123,826	$250,722	$459,714	$803,931

In this category in the *GRAND SUMMARY* of possible growth of money we have used a savings of $150 per month with growth to $229,857 in 40 years.

LOTTERIES AND GAMBLING

Refer as necessary to the chapter on Lotteries and Gambling, page 153.

The following figures represent dollars some people *spend* each month with very big odds against their winning compared to the certain amounts they would gain by *depositing* the amounts, compounded each month at 5 percent annual rate.

Monthly savings and deposit	Will grow to these amounts in the years indicated				
	10 years	20 years	30 years	40 years	50 years
$5	$780	$2,064	$4,179	$7,662	$13,399
$10	$1,560	$4,128	$8,358	$15,324	$26,798
$15	$2,340	$6,192	$12,537	$22,986	$40,197
$20	$3,120	$8,256	$16,716	$30,648	$53,596
$25	$3,900	$10,320	$20,895	$38,310	$66,995
$50	$7,800	$20,640	$41,790	$76,620	$133,990
$100	$15,600	$41,280	$83,580	$153,240	$267,980

In this category in the *GRAND SUMMARY* of possible growth of money we have used a savings of $20 per month with growth to $30,648 in 40 years.

CREDIT CARD DEBT

Refer as necessary to the chapter on Credit Cards, page 159.

These savings are based on the decrease or elimination of monthly credit card debt, at 18 percent per year on balances due, and the depositing of the amount of the savings each month at 5 percent per year compounded monthly.

Monthly savings and deposit	Will grow to these amounts in the years indicated				
	10 years	20 years	30 years	40 years	50 years
$25	$3,898	$10,319	$20,893	$38,309	$66,994
$50	$7,796	$20,638	$41,787	$76,619	$133,989
$75	$11,695	$30,956	$62,680	$114,928	$200,983
$100	$15,593	$41,275	$83,574	$153,238	$267,977
$200	$31,186	$82,551	$167,148	$306,476	$535,954
$300	$46,779	$123,826	$250,722	$459,714	$803,931
$400	$62,372	$165,101	$334,295	$612,951	$1,071,908
$500	$77,965	$206,377	$417,869	$766,189	$1,339,886

In this category in the GRAND SUMMARY of possible growth of money we have used a savings of $100 per month with growth to $153,238 in 40 years.

It is important you understand that your savings and investment plans cannot all be put into effect immediately. Some can, but some may take months or years before putting them into effect. Do plan to put them into effect as soon as possible.

It is important you start at the earliest possible age. If you build or buy a house larger than necessary or drive cars more expensive than necessary, it might take a few or several years to put that part of your savings plans into effect.

The ability to save money depends on cutting some expenses or increasing your income to provide the money to be deposited and invested.

We have attempted to present the more probable sources of funds that can be saved and deposited. As you develop your system, be constantly mindful that the funds to be saved and deposited have to come from some action on your part.

If you have already made some mistakes on housing and automobiles, for example, you may have to plan to adjust those expenses downward, when convenient, to make possible the savings you wish to accomplish.

The present payment on your home mortgage may not leave any separate dollars for investing. If so, you may need to continue the large payments on your mortgage until you make a substantial reduction in it.

310

At that time you might refinance your mortgage with lower payments over extended years. This would give you the opportunity to save and invest the extra dollars. There may be a question whether it is better to make additional payments on a mortgage on which you are paying $8 \, 1/2$ percent than to invest that amount of money in a separate savings account earning 5 percent interest. Your tax counselor can assist you in making the decision which is best for you.

In the case of automobiles the opportunity to generate cash and savings probably will come easier when you buy a new car and move from premium to mid-premium or from mid-premium to a lower level. The monthly savings in finance charges and insurance will provide the savings and cash to start this money-saving opportunity.

The "bottom line," as they say in business, depends on cutting some expenses to provide the cash for savings and investing.

In Chapter 1 of this book we presented a chart reminding you of rewards that can be yours. We gave examples of six dollar amounts that can be yours in *40 years* and will now identify them.

— The $34,812 represents one can of pop a day.

— The $195,378 represents one pack of cigarettes a day.

— The $76,619 represents saving $50 per month on groceries.

311

— The $153,238 represents paying $100 per month less interest on credit card debt.

— The $306,471 represents saving $200 per month on a home mortgage.

Here are additional examples of other savings that will grow in 40 years.

— $20 monthly saved by not buying lottery tickets or gambling will grow to $30,648.

— $100 less spending per month on Hobbies, Entertainment and a Big Etc. will grow to $153,238.

— A savings of $225,260 on purchasing and operating automobiles.

You will note in the following *GRAND SUMMARY* of savings and money growth we have presented four monthly savings of less than $100. One at $20.00, one at $22.50 and two at $50.00. If some of the monthly suggested savings seem too difficult for you these small monthly savings to a total of $218,698 will encourage you to do the very best you can!

The *GRAND SUMMARY* does not include many other types of expenses where money can be saved and grow.

Think of other small savings you can achieve per month. Then refer to the Master Chart on Compounding in CHAPTER 1 to get the figures on what these savings will grow to in 40 years.

THE GRAND SUMMARY		
ITEM	AMOUNT SAVED MONTHLY	WILL GROW TO THIS AMOUNT IN 40 YEARS
POP	$22.50	$34,812
CIGARETTES	$127.50	$195,378
GROCERIES	$50.00	$76,619
CREDIT CARDS	$100.00	$153,238
HOUSING	$200.00	$306,476
CARPOOLING	$50.00	$76,619
AUTOMOBILES	$147.00	$225,260
LOTTERY AND GAMBLING	$20.00	$30,648
HOBBIES AND ENTERTAINMENT	$150.00	$229,857

A GRAND TOTAL OF $1,328,907!

Who said you couldn't become a millionaire?

Plan and *you can* do it in *your lifetime!*

Dollars are great, but their importance lies in the security and happiness they provide.